UNDERSTANDING AMERICAN AND GERMAN BUSINESS CULTURES

A manager's guide to the cultural context

in which American and German companies operate

Revised Third Edition

Patrick L. Schmidt

GERMAN AMERICAN CHAMBER OF COMMERCE INC.

NEW YORK

Printed in Canada

Canadian Cataloguing in Publishing Data

Schmidt, Patrick L., 1949-

Understanding American and German Business Cultures: a manager's guide to the cultural context in which American and German companies operate

Includes bibliographical references and index.
ISBN 0-9685293-0-5

1. Corporate culture — Germany —Cross-cultural studies. 2. Corporate culture — United States — Cross-cultural studies. 3. National characteristics, Germans. 4. National characteristics, Americans I.Title

HD58.7.S3435 1999   302.3'5'0943   C99-900822-6

Book cover design by Laurent Michelot

The German version of the book is published by Hainholz Verlag (www.hainholz.de) with the title
"Die amerikanische und die deutsche Wirtschaftskultur im Vergleich"

Understanding American and German business Cultures —
A Manager's guide to the Cultural Context in which American and German Companies operate
was originally published by Merdian World Press in 1999.

Quantity discounts are available on bulk purchases of this book for training purposes. For information, contact:

GERMAN AMERICAN CHAMBER OF COMMERCE INC.
40 West 57th Street, 31 st Floor
New York, NY 10019-4092
Tel: (212) 974-8830 Fax: (212) 974-8867

Xmas 06

Dear Bjorn,
    HAVE a great experience in Germany
and tell me all about it! Love,
                                    Uncle Rick

This book is dedicated to my wife

Jacqueline

who provided unfailing support and encouragement
throughout its writing.

TABLE OF CONTENTS

Acknowledgments

This book is an outgrowth of the support of many people who urged me to write about my intercultural experiences in Germany. I wish to thank the following persons for their contributions, assistance and patience.

Professor Nancy Adler of McGill University, who gave me the initial encouragement to undertake this project. Jennifer Flechsenhar and Vinita Balasubramanian, my faithful senior editors who provided excellent cultural insights and whose suggestions demonstrated great knowledge of German culture. Anthony Curtis for offering intelligent criticism mixed with remarkable sensitivity. Dan MacLeod for editing the text into a tight piece of prose.

Additionally, I wish to acknowledge the following reviewers who read through various drafts and provided detailed, thoughtful and useful comments: Gunhild Berendsen, Jacques Bourque, Neville Cloutier, Hans Jensen, Ralph Rogers, Suzanne Hill, Michael and Elisabeth Morris, Wolfgang Hartung and Wolfram Havemann.

Patrick Schmidt
Montreal, Canada

Introduction

The Need for Intercultural Sensitivity

"The Germans are just too obsessed about doing things perfectly. If this keeps up, our operations here will go bankrupt."

American manufacturing executive, working in Frankfurt

"The Americans are very easy-going and self-confident. But behind that facade, we often find them shallow. They don't always follow up on what they say they are going to do."

German engineering executive, working in Los Angeles

The two quotes above illustrate clearly the stress and frustration international executives often feel when trying to cope with another culture. Each country has its own way of perceiving and doing things, with subconscious assumptions that can make cooperation difficult. Learning to live in a new environment is, in most cases, a painful process of adapting to unstated rules and hidden differences. Communications sometimes seem to break down and it is then that something in human nature prompts us to have negative feelings toward anybody who is not "one of us". Judgmental and condescending remarks, like those expressed above, are often the result.

How does one overcome intercultural misunderstandings? Curiously, the basis of any successful overseas adaptation is not so much learning about a new culture as it is acquiring a better understanding of your *own* background. This becomes apparent when you arrive in a foreign country for the first time. Nothing is more startling than to realize how much your work and leisure habits, your taste in food, even your outlook on life continue to depend on values learned in childhood. Only by becoming aware of your own "cultural baggage" will it be possible to transcend your thought-patterns so that, in the end, you'll be able to comprehend "foreign behavior".

The premise of this book is simple: understanding your culture and your own "mental software" is a prerequisite to understanding other people's ways and habits. By explaining the psychology and behavior of Americans* and Germans respectively, both American and German readers will become conscious of their own national uniqueness. This book doesn't pretend to solve the problems of cultural transition, but attempts to anticipate them by explaining the context in which American and German firms operate.

The work is divided into seven chapters, the first of which discusses the concept of culture and how social scientists have designed theoretical frameworks to explain behavioral differences. These frameworks will contribute to an initial understanding of how culture operates and allow the reader to better understand the ways in which German and American companies differ.

The chapters which follow describe the behavioral patterns of Americans and Germans, first from a psychological point of view, then with a look at business practices, communication, and the influences of the respective legal systems. Lastly, the book attempts to describe the characteristics of an interculturally-competent person.

For the most part, the comparative method is used. A basic example is the fact that a German speech is normally longer, very detailed and more serious, quite different from the standard American presentation which is shorter, humorous and with easy to remember statements. Contrasting has the advantage of reducing our reliance on a single set of values; it challenges the implicit superiority of one culture over another.

Although every culture has its collective qualities, its members are individuals and there are always exceptions to the rule. Many readers might say that generalizations of national traits through the use of clichés and stereotypes can be misleading. Despite this, the author firmly believes that each culture is a unified entity, in which everything interrelates. An "inherent logic" can be discovered through close observation.

Becoming interculturally sensitive and competent is much like learning a foreign language: it takes practice and continual intellectual effort. But it offers unexpected and pleasant rewards. By understanding the sometimes obscure codes of another culture and their impact on behavior, you learn much more about *yourself*. This is, in the last analysis, what makes intercultural learning so attractive. If this book encourages the reader to view and analyze cultural differences in terms of "why I act in the way I do", it will have succeeded in its mission.

---

*) "Americans" in this book, for purposes of clarity and simplicity, refers to the predominately white, middle-class mainstream.

Chapter 1

The Concept of Culture

Unusual Behavior

Imagine a small village, located somewhere in the northern hemisphere. A man is sitting in front of his house while his wife prepares dinner. She goes out to draw water from the local well. There, she meets a charming young man and takes him back to meet her husband. They chat pleasantly for a while and the husband invites the young man for dinner.

After the meal, the husband goes to bed, leaving his wife alone with their guest. Later, she invites the guest to sleep with her.

The next morning, the husband gets up to prepare breakfast and calls his wife and guest to eat. The three have breakfast together and, afterward, the young man thanks the couple for their warm hospitality and continues on his travels.

Unusual behavior? Not in the Ammassalik Eskimo culture, where hospitality to a guest means offering one's wife for the night.

This story illustrates how people from different countries have their own ways and customs of dealing with day-to-day life, often based on unstated rules. The hidden differences are what many refer to as culture.

What is culture? *Webster's New World Dictionary* gives five different definitions of the word:

1. the cultivation of the soil;
2. production, development or improvement of a particular plant, animal, commodity;
3. the literature, art, music and architecture of a given country;
4. development, improvement or refinement of the mind, emotions, interests, manners, tastes;
5. the ideas, customs, skills, arts, etc. of a given people, transmitted from generation to generation.

The last definition is what we shall examine. Culture is, as the social researcher G.P. Ferraro said, "everything that people have, think, and do as members of society."

How do we acquire culture? All of us receive specific training through the process called socialization. We learn "correct behavior" from our families, friends, schools, religious institutions and even from TV commercials. Learning your mother tongue is also a signifiant part of this process. Language embodies the "mentality", the cultural environment.

As the socialization process is (for the most part) not explicit, attempting to grasp and articulate one's own culture is a formidable task. Culture is so much a part of us that, when we're asked to identify it, we find the ideas difficult to express. Cultural behavior is so well *ingrained* in people's minds that they can't imagine their lifestyle as being otherwise.

A useful metaphor for culture is that it's what water is to a fish. The fish takes water for granted. Take it out of its environment, however, and the fish suddenly realizes it needs water to survive.

The same applies to us. We're not really aware of our own culture until we bump into another one. The meeting of two different "patterns of thinking" inevitably results in conflict, disorientation and disagreement. The story of Eskimo hospitality shows the extent to which cultures may differ in degree on a shared concept.

Another useful metaphor is to compare the term *culture* with an iceberg. Certain aspects are obvious, just as the tip of an iceberg is visible. These are what we refer to as *observable elements* — the level of conscious awareness. They represent the first contacts with a new culture, such as language, dress, customs, habits, etc. For example, the Swabian people in southwest Germany have a long tradition of *Kehrwoche* (sweeping week), where tradition dictates that everyone sweeps the path to their doorway, usually on a Saturday. *Kehrwoche* obviously expresses the Swabian need to have everything spic and span but, although highly visible, it provides only a superficial understanding of the society.

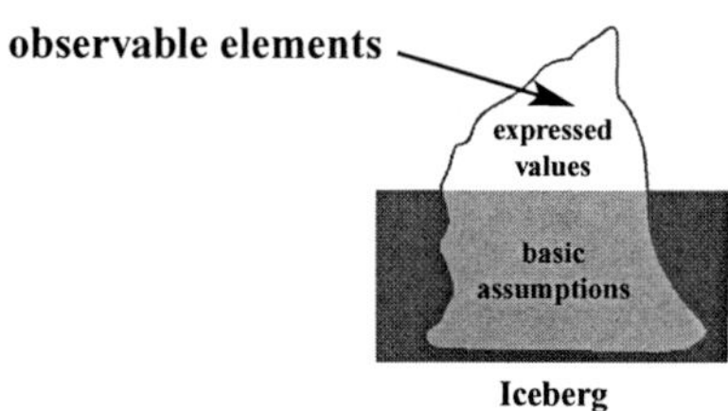

Iceberg

The most significant elements that provide a deeper comprehension of culture are unseen. They are basic, unspoken assumptions, the core values which guide people's thoughts and actions. Coming back to *Kehrwoche*, sweeping symbolically brings a feeling of orderliness, a central theme in German thinking and actions. Less obvious is the reason behind this "value" which is, in fact, a need.

Another example of basic assumptions is how American and German mentalities differ with regard to age in the workplace. In the U.S., where youth and energy are highly valued, most companies avoid hiring anybody over 40. Such a person is seen as too old to start anew. Germans, however, value qualifications and experience. A 35-year-old is perceived as someone who's still learning. A person of 50 is said to be in his or her prime. The unspoken belief is that age provides wisdom and, more importantly, that wisdom is superior to "drive".

CLASSIFYING CULTURES THROUGH THEORETICAL FRAMEWORKS

Social researchers have designed theoretical frameworks to explain why people from different countries do things in different ways. These structures are averages or norms of the value systems that make up a culture; they are not meant to be exact. The reader is provided with an approximate idea what behavioral tendencies to expect in different cultures. It should be pointed out that none of the theories are considered to be absolutely correct or better than the others, but should be viewed as tools, practical methods for "reading" and understanding a culture.

We shall examine the theoretical frameworks of Geert Hofstede, a Dutch social researcher and Edward T. Hall, an American anthropologist.

Hofstede's Dimensions of Work-Related Values

In 1980, Geert Hofstede published a fascinating study on work-related values and attitudes based on data he collected from IBM employees. Over 116,000 employees' habits throughout the world were analyzed. Because the employees came from the same company, the differences can be reliably attributed to national culture.

Hofstede extracted four dimensions of values to explain differences in behavior:

1. individualism/collectivism,
2. power distance,
3. uncertainty avoidance,
4. masculinity/femininity.

By using the average scores for each country, he generated national profiles that explained differences in work habits.

Individualism/Collectivism: Hofstede defined **individualistic** countries as nations where people are more concerned for themselves and their families than for others. Short, a "me" society. Each person's rights are valued and organizational systems attempt to honor individual preference and choice. An employee's evaluation is based on individually agreed-upon objectives.

Collectivist cultures place a high value on the overall good of the group. People subordinate individual interests and needs for common benefit. It's a "we" society. In exchange for loyalty, people look after each other, emphasize belonging to the group, and make collective decisions.

Power Distance is defined as the extent to which lesser members of a group accept that power is unequally distributed. A society with a **small power distance** is not comfortable with social class or company ranking. For example, in Austria, there is more participation in decision-making and somewhat more disregard for hierarchical level than in Germany.

In a **large power distance culture**, people with different standings are accepted. The individual's position in society influences how that person will act and, conversely, how others treat him or her. Someone with a high-level rank shows a certain respect for inferiors, however differences of status are always present. If a manager were to delegate decision-making to a subordinate, it would imply that the manager is unable to make the decisions himself. In a large power distance country such as Singapore, managers tend to be autocratic or paternalistic.

In figure 1 (page 11), Hofstede compared individualism/collectivism with power distance. What is interesting from a German-American perspective is that the chart shows that Germans (35), as well as the Swiss (34) and the Austrians (11), have a smaller power distance score than the Americans (40), but the Americans are much more individualistic than the Germans (91 to 67).

Uncertainty Avoidance (page 12, figure 2): This value indicates the preferred amount of structure in a society. In a strong uncertainty avoidance country there are more rigid rules of behavior, both written and unwritten. Correspondingly, laws are stricter and penalties heavier. Officials and experts are admired, seldom questioned. Emphasis is on doing things correctly and people won't start a new project without doing thorough research.

At the other extreme, **weak uncertainty avoidance** cultures tend to be comfortable with unstructured situations. Organizations are more flexible and people more easy-going and creative.

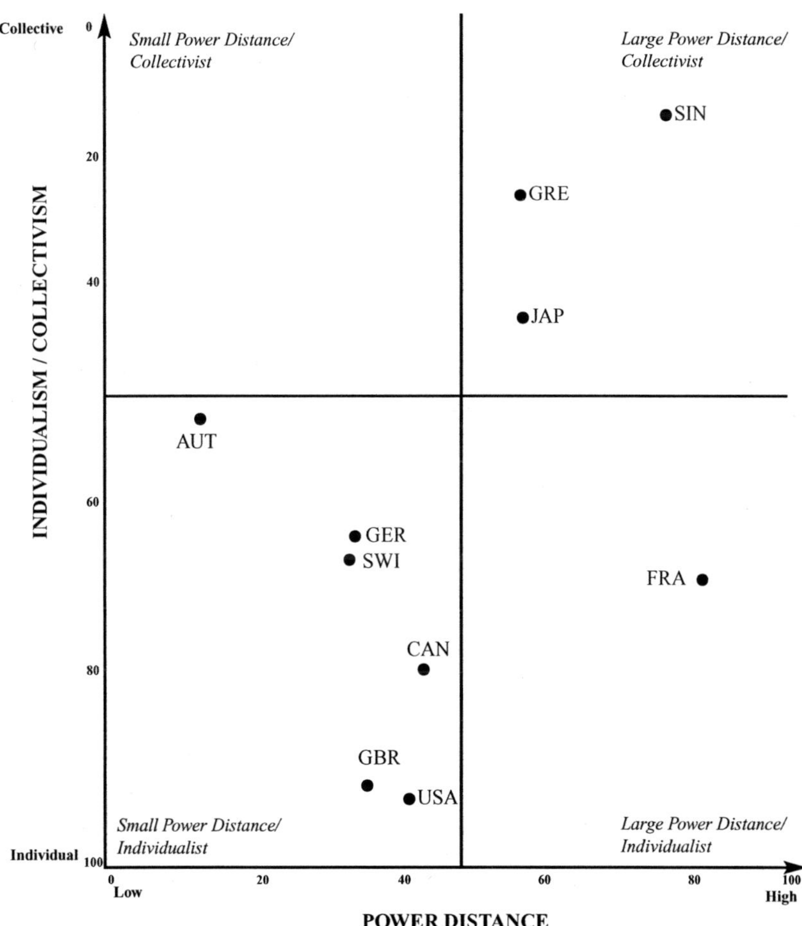

Figure 1 — Hofstede's Dimensions of Cultural Values Illustrated

Source: Adapted from Geert Hofstede's "Positions of Forty Countries on Power Distance and Individualism" from *Organizational Dynamics*, Summer 1980. Reprinted by permission of the author.

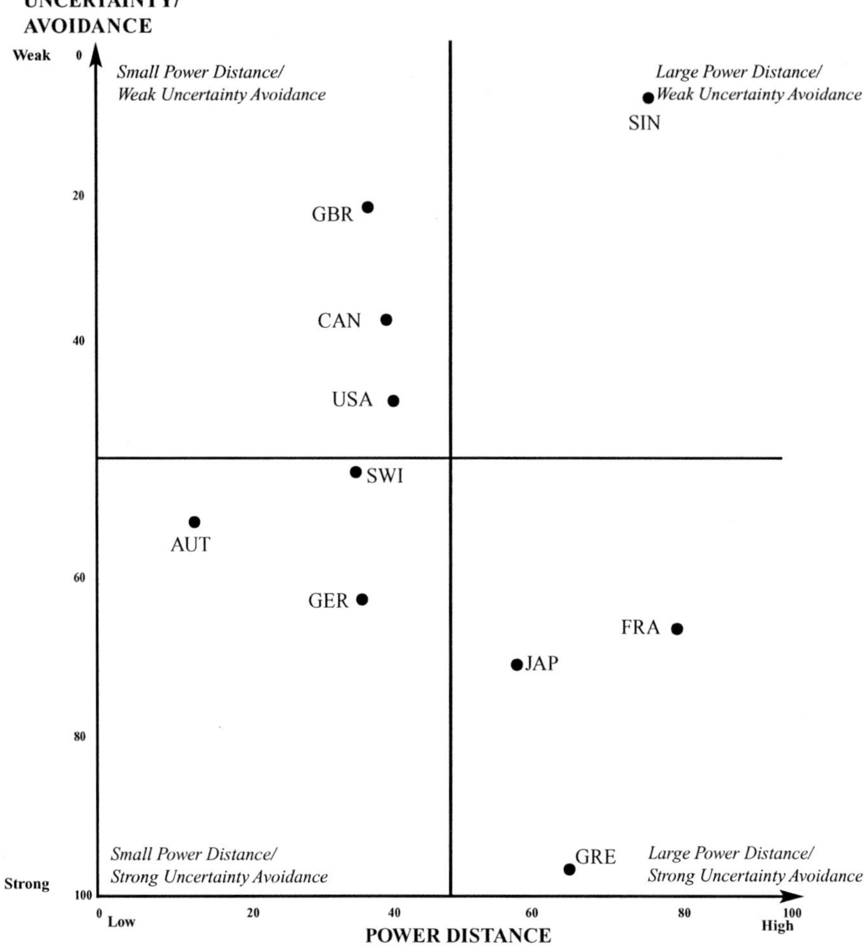

Figure 2 — Hofstede's Dimensions of Cultural Values Illustrated *(continued)*

Comparing Americans and Germans, the former show less need for uncertainty avoidance (46 to 65), meaning they have stronger feelings of personal competency and a more entrepreneurial spirit.

Masculinity/Femininity (page 13, figure 3): Hofstede defines a **masculine** society as being dominated by "tough" values, such as money, success, assertiveness and competition. Men and women often have significantly different roles. Japan scored an extremely high masculine value because the culture

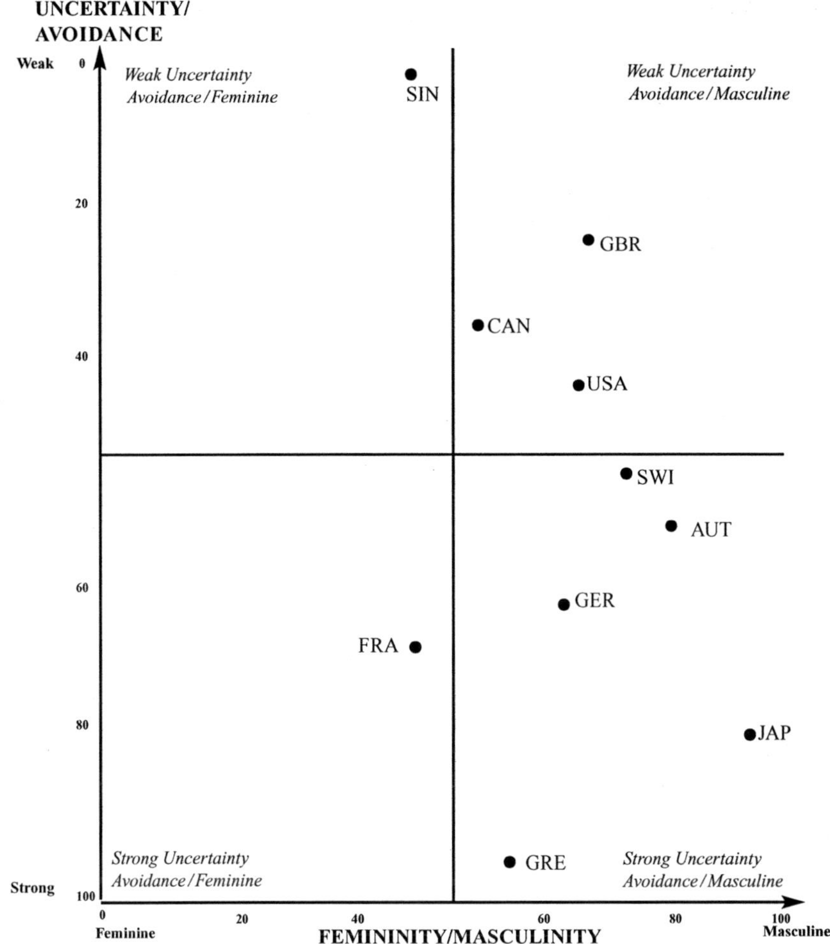

Figure 3 — Hofstede's Dimensions of Cultural Values Illustrated *(continued)*

values earnings, recognition, advancement and challenge.

A **feminine** culture puts emphasis on "tender" values such as relationships, care for others, quality of life and service. Men's and women's roles are less distinct and often equal. Norway and Sweden score high in feminine value by preferring cooperation, a friendly environment, security of employment and group decision-making.

This last chart makes clear that both the USA and Germany have approximately the same masculine characteristics (62 to 66 respectively).

Hofstede's study demonstrates that:
- work-related values are *not* universal;
- national cultural values are likely to persist, even when a multinational tries to impose the same norms on all its branches;
- local values will determine how head office's regulations are interpreted.

Hall's High- and Low-Context Cultural Framework

The American anthropologist, Edward Hall, approaches the understanding of cultures through communication. He defines culture as "a system for creating, sending, storing and processing information. The common thread that runs through all cultures is communication." How people communicate depends on *context* , "the information that surrounds an event; it is inextricably bound up with the meaning of that event".

Hall worked out groundbreaking concepts in the different ways we experience the world. He classifies cultures on a scale of low- to high-context. In a high-context society, communication is implicit: coded, circular, indirect. The message comes not only through words, but also through body language, the surroundings, the relationship between the people involved.

For example, the Japanese would never reject an American offer with a straight "no" because Japanese cultures values face-saving. Whem the Japanese say "We shall give it some consideration", the contextual meaning is the equivalent of the American "no", A high context communicator is sensitive to situational or contextual data, i.e. implicit information. *The priority is to avoid giving offense by being relationship and feeling-focused. It is feminine in nature.*

Hall cites the Arab, Japanese, and Mediterranean peoples as high-context cultures, having close personal relationships and extensive information networks. People are interrupting constantly, coming and going, giving and taking information. In the workplace of a high-context country information flows freely from all sides. The manager usually keeps the door to his office open. This results in everyone being relatively informed about all aspects of the business.

People in low-context cultures — such as Americans, Germans, Swiss, and Scandinavians — don't place so much importance on context in a conversation. Communication is explicit: direct, clear, linear, verbal. Words don't need to be interpreted through the understanding of the culture, but are straightforward and more blunt. "No" means no and "yes" means yes. *The priority is clarity by being result- and thinking- focused. It is masculine in nature.*

A low-context culture compartmentalizes personal relationships, work, and many aspects of day-to-day life. An American or German executive office is a closed room, a sort of hideaway for the boss that keeps distractions at a distance. Information communicated in the office is shared only with a select few. The result is a lack of extensive, well-developed information networks outside one's own special area of expertise. Compartmentalization means people need to receive more detailed and explicit information before making a decision.

Monochronic and Polychronic Societies

Another important aspect of culture, according to Hall, is that of time. He points out that there are two types of time important to international business, monochronic and polychronic.

In a monochronic society, people concentrate on one activity at a time. Time is linear and can be divided into segments, compartmentalized. A schedule has an extremely high value and is sometimes seen as almost sacred.

Both the U.S. and Germany are classified as monochronic countries. Time is talked about as if it were a real, tangible object. "Time is money" sends out the message that it can be "spent," "saved," "wasted," and "lost." An American businessman might say "If I do a Berlitz crash-course in German, after 40 hours I will have learned $2,500 worth of German." As absurd as this may be, it's the way he perceives reality.

Monochronic time is so ingrained in German and American thinking patterns that the large majority of people think it's nature-based. In fact, it is conditioned behavior, which grew out of the industrial revolution in England. The factory required its labor force to be in place at a scheduled time.

While a monochronic lifestyle appears to increase efficiency, it violates our biological rhythms. A more natural way of being is the polychronic system, characterized by the simultaneous occurrence of many activities, more emphasis on people and relationships than on holding to schedules. For example, two Italian businessmen are more likely to continue a highly-animated conversation than to stop abruptly because of upcoming appointments. The emphasis is on actual activity rather than pre-made plans. Latin countries such as France, Spain and Italy are characterized as polychronic cultures.

The theories of Hofstede and Hall show how frameworks can help explain cultural differences and their relation to organizational behavior. They provide insights as to why people behave the way they do, as we shall see in the following chapters.

Discussion Questions

1. What is culture? How is it a useful concept in studying German and American business behavior?

2. Think about your own culture. Are you aware of the socialization processes that took place in your childhood? How do you think the values and behavior you were taught early in life affect your behavior now?

3. Using the illustrations of Hofstede's dimensions of values (individualism/ collectivism, power distance, uncertainty avoidance and masculinity/ femininity), try to describe what you think the French, Singaporian, and Greek cultures are like.

4. How does the studying and understanding the concept of culture make you a better manager overall?

Chapter 2

United States of America and Federal Republic of Germany:

A Statistical Comparison

	USA	Germany
Total Land Area	9,363,520 sq. km.	357,621 sq. km.
Size Comparison	World's 4th largest country, between Canada and Brazil	Slightly larger than the state of New Mexico
Coastline	19,144 km	2,216 km
Land Use	20% arable 26% meadows 29% forest and woods	34% arable 17% meadows 29% forest and woods
Largest Cities	New York: 7,325,000 Los Angeles: 3,500,000 Chicago: 2,800,000 Houston: 1,650,000	Berlin: 3,410,000 Hamburg: 1,630,000 Munich: 1,210,000 Cologne: 950,000
Population (2004)	293,000,000	82,400,000
Population Density	29 per sq. km.	230 per sq. km.
Urban Dwellers	76%	82%
Ethnic Groups	white: 75% black: 12% hispanic: 9% Asian/Pacific: 3% American Indian/Eskimo: 1%	Germans: 92% Foreigners: 8%
Major Religions	Protestant: 56% Roman Catholic: 28% Jewish: 2%	Protestant: 45% Roman Catholic: 37%
Life expectancy at birth	72.9 males, 79.6 females	73.8 males, 80.3 females
GNP (2004)	US $ 11.4 trillion[1]	US $ 2.64 trillion[2]
Per capital annual income	US $ 37,800	US $ 32,050
Import (2004) Export (2004)	US $ 1,764 billion[1] US $ 1,146 billion[1]	US $ 750 billion[2] US $ 953 billion[2]

1) U.S. Census Bureau   2) Statistisches Bundesamt Deutschland

The Psychology of Germans and Americans

"The Germans make everything difficult, both for themselves and for everyone else."

Johann Wolfgang von Goethe (1749-1832)

"The American dream is often a very private dream of being the star, the uniquely successful and admirable one, the one who stands out from the crowd of ordinary folk who don't know how."

from the collection *Habits of the Heart* (1986)

When describing a culture, we also refer to the *psychology of a people*, i.e. their mental and emotional processes. This leads to an interesting question: why have groups chosen different values and norms, leading to different cultures? The answer can be found by going into that innate part of thoughts, knowns as "basic assumptions".

The strongest basic assumption of any group is to survive, which means fighting every day against nature. The Dutch against the mounting sea, the Swiss against the Alps and avalanches, the Eskimos against intense cold. Today, in post-industrial societies, it is the struggle to obtain a proper education and suitable employment. Every group tries its best to deal with its environment according to its means.

Over the centuries, permanent problems have found solutions wherein our actions are automatic, unconscious. Accepting the fact that much of our behavior is subconscious, the meeting of two cultures can lead to a lot of confusion. To understand subtle differences in a new culture, one needs to study their historic origins.

This chapter attempts to describe historical factors and the psychological make-up of Germans and Americans which have made these two nations the way they are. The comparative method will be used so that the reader can immediately grasp where the differences are.

A note to the reader: Every culture has a close balance between positive and negative characteristics. Some of the national traits of the Americans and Germans presented in this book may appear harsh, rousing strong feelings. The author wishes to emphasize that they aren't pointed out in order to criticize. Rather, they allow us to see ourselves from a cross-cultural perspective, which can provide a strikingly original view of one's reality.

To accept one's own culture, warts and all, can be difficult. Hopefully, the reader will understand these contrasts as a manner of viewing his or her culture in its full dimension. To know ourselves better is to grow.

The Historical Origins of the German Character

Much of what we now call "typically German", i.e. perfection and need for order, can be attributed in large part to a relatively dreadful past. As any psychiatrist or psychologist will tell you, a child who has been traumatized will often take the route of perfectionism as an adult to avoid feeling worthless. The same could be extrapolated to the nation of Germany.

American historian Gordon A. Craig, in his book *The Germans*, points out that the country has suffered more than its share of wartime horror, beginning with the Thirty Years War (1618-1648). This religious conflict was a gigantic duel between Austria and Spain, on the one hand, and France, Sweden, Holland and Denmark on the other. The majority of the battlefields, in which their struggle for mastery was played out, were in Germany. The German people had the misfortune of being *das Land der Mitte*, the country in the middle.

The consequences were horrendous. By 1641, the population of Württemberg had been reduced from 400,000 to 48,000 and its northern neighbor, the Palatinate, had lost 80% of its people. Likewise, physical property was ruthlessly destroyed. Swedish troops alone demolished 18,000 villages in the last years of the war, along with 1500 towns and 200 castles.

Despite the fact that northern and eastern Germany — Upper and Lower Saxony, Holstein, Oldenburg, Hamburg and Prussia — were relatively untouched by the war, the country as a whole lost about 35% of its population, falling from 21 million people to about 13.5 million (along with immense destruction of property). The terrible psychological and social toll the Germans suffered could only have a profound impact on the generations to come.

And other tragic conflicts were to follow: the Napoleonic Wars, the Austro-Prussian War, then two World Wars. In the last of these, the Holocaust, brought disgrace and shame upon the German people as a whole.

Not only was there mass destruction and death, but also massive financial losses. Runaway inflation wiped out the middle class in the '20s. The currency reform of 1948 meant the Reichsmark lost 90% of its value in just one day.

Given Germany's tragic and violent past, it's not surprising that wars and their consequences have played a large role in the German *Angst* towards uncertainty and the need for order.

Historical Analysis of the American Character

Studying the social and historical background of America, you will find that what has made the country unique from previous civilizations is the profound belief that it is the "land of the free". Free to be and to do what one wants.

This idea has attracted millions of immigrants from all parts of the world, resulting in a rich culture of European, African, Latin American, Asian and Arab influences. However, the country derives its roots from Anglo-Saxon culture.

The U.S. was founded by northern European settlers, mostly from Great Britain, fleeing religious persecution. They brought a rejection of traditions, skepticism toward the Old World, and enthusiasm for new ideas. One in particular was Jean-Jacques Rousseau's philosophy that if man decided to believe in the good of others, society would become highly efficient and dynamic. Mutual trust would eliminate the heavy, time-consuming process of doubting and judging. It was exactly what America needed to develop itself. When building a nation, decisions have to be made quickly. "Yes or no" became the norm. "Time is money".

This simplistic notion of life — which ignored the complexities and nuances that existence continually presents — created the American traits of being unsentimental and without traditional standards of behavior. It was part of breaking away from the past and marching into the unknown with confidence and hope.

Perhaps what makes the Americans seem so nonchalant and happy-go-lucky is that the country hasn't experienced the massive losses of life that have so marked Europe throughout history. The United States suffered only one real tragedy, the American Civil War. In that four-year conflict, 600,000 soldiers were killed. Out of a population of 30 million at the time, that was a relatively high toll: two percent of the nation. World War II casualties were nothing like the nightmare of 1861-65. The number of American soldiers killed between 1941-45 (300,000 in a population of 150 million) represented only two tenths of one percent.

German losses during WW II were much higher. Over 3.5 million soldiers and

and 780,000 civilians were killed, a total of almost 4.3 million people. Of a population of 70 million, 6.5% lost their lives. Human tragedy strikes closer to the German soul than that of the American.

With rich natural resources, "Yankee ingenuity" for being shrewd and productive while conquering new challenges, and the lack of any real historical tragedy, the U.S. flourished. Thus, an oversimplified trust in humanity blended with a belief in the "pursuit of happiness". It's no wonder that America transformed itself into the most powerful country in the world. Anyone could evolve from "rags to riches", it was said, and millions of poor immigrants moved up the social ladder. All these elements were the seeds that gave birth to the myth of the "happy ending".

This is reflected in many American movies, which convey the simplistic message "the good guys win and the bad guys lose". When a complicated human problem presents itself, Americans often refuse to see it, the result of their traditional belief in the superficial good of everything.

Consequently, an oversimplified attitude towards life forms the present character. Americans, as a whole, don't radiate a healthy human skepticism and deep thinking which give the elements of a full-rounded person. It's no surprise that so many people perceive Americans as somewhat naive and superficial, too light-hearted to be earnest.

Psychological Characteristics of Germans and Americans

The German need to be *ernsthaft* (serious) and *ordentlich* (orderly) versus American self-confidence and the "sunny boy" image

A desire for security lies at the core of German culture, expressed so well by the axiom *Ordnung muß sein* (there must be order). The Germans, simply put, have an extremely low threshold for uncertainty. To counteract this unconscious feeling, they strive to be serious and extremely well-organized.

This *Ordnung* behavior manifests itself everywhere. Foreigners who arrive in Germany for the first time are surprised by the German need to do everything perfectly and correctly. Almost nothing is improvised. Listening to the German news on the radio is an example. The announcer speaks in a steady monotone, appearing to display absolutely no emotion. No matter what may be happening in the world, order remains.

Ordnung best expresses itself in the excessive number of rules and regulations in the country. Almost every aspect of daily life is controlled and much is *verboten* (forbidden). "Quiet time" laws state that no noise of any kind is allowed between 1:30 and 3:30 in the afternoon, as well as all day long on Sunday. (The author, living in Stuttgart, once attempted to mow the lawn late one Sunday morning. Within ten minutes the police arrived to say that two laws were being broken: the one barring manual labor on Sunday and the one prohibiting noise.)

However, this extreme sense of order leads Germans to be rational, disciplined and industrious. As *Time* magazine once noted, they are brilliant organizers and planners who like complexity and are good at integrating things, including people, into a big system. All these combined traits have contributed in making Germany a much-respected and rich nation.

Germans don't spend too much time on foolishness or jokes. The French writer Stendhal summed this up in 1820: "It seems to me that more jokes are said in Paris in one evening than in all of Germany in one month." Germans have a sense of humor, but generally prefer to express it in their private life. They don't mix business and humor until they're sure their counterparts will be able to take them seriously. And they don't go in for is self-deprecating humor, i.e. making fun about their own weaknesses.

Their seriousness explains why Germany is not known as a "smiling nation" — life and work are strict business. This soberness can be experienced in German films such as *The White Rose, Stalingrad, Das Boot, The Tin Drum* and *The Downfall*. This doesn't mean Germans are unfriendly; they're simply more reserved, keeping their emotions to themselves. For example, at a social gathering, Germans often have difficulty in making "small talk".

Another important German trait is their desire to be fair and above all decent (*brav*) at all times and all cost. "If you want the world to be orderly, you need to be fair." Germans in any form of contest — whether it be in business, sports or personal relationships — generally don't cheat. This is not to say they never foul. They will resort to unfair play only after they have repeatedly been fouled against.

The common expression *Durchsetzungsvermögen* (power to assert oneself) helps explain German persistence in striving for perfection, sometimes seen as arrogance by foreigners. When Germans decide upon a certain course of action, they apply themselves 100% and won't stop until they've attained their goal. This has resulted in phenomenal success in business, especially in export-oriented industries. Despite a severe lack of natural resources, Germany exports approximately $11,600 per capita, as compared to $3,900 for the U.S. (from Statistisches Bundesamt Deutschland and U.S. Census Bureau, 2004).

Closely related to the need for order is their vision of what is right and wrong. When they come across a situation that inadvertently violates habits or social customs, Germans — especially the older generation — will not hesitate to lecture people. Non-respect for the order of things makes them anxious and uneasy. Often, this striving for perfection tends to make them feel they "know better" than non-Germans, leading foreigners to perceive them sometimes as haughty.

Although Germans appear highly disciplined, they possess a childlike romanticism within themselves. The language mirrors this in the common expression: *Ich habe mich gefreut wie ein Kind.* (I was as delighted as a child). Longing for an ideal world allows them to escape into what the poet Heinrich Heine (1797-1856) called "the airy realm of dreams". And romanticism explains, in part, why Germans are such relentless tourists. Being perfectionists and idealists, they are searching for an ideal country. From a psychological point of view, *Schwärmerei* (daydreaming) and *Wanderlust* (a longing to travel) are reactions against societal demands that Germans must always be serious and orderly!

The Americans are just the opposite in how they project themselves. Despite the fact that Americans share the same cultural values as Germans (predominantly monochronic, low-context), the former exhibit a "sunny-boy outlook": that combination of openness, friendliness, optimism, vitality and spontaneity. These characteristics are so unique you can usually pick out an American anywhere in the world.

Americans are raised with the idea that everyone has the right to express their individuality ("individual freedom"). They are taught not to recognize their places in the social order and to constantly assert themselves. Americans consider themselves as individuals first, and only secondarily as members of a family, organization or religion. This baffles people from cultures in which one's identity is, for the most part, an extension of his or her family.

Alan Roland, in his book *In Search of Self in India and Japan*, psychoanalyzed Americans, Indians and Japanese. He found that the two Asian cultures had absolutely no notion of the "inner separation" from others that is so typical of Americans. The author concluded that Americans displayed "a militant individualism, combined with enormous social mobility", permitting very little group identity.

Paradoxically, although individualism plays an important part in their psyche, there is strong pressure in American culture to conform and be liked. In 1835 the French aristocrat Alexis de Tocqueville observed this need for conformity in his brilliant classic *Democracy in America*. He noted that, while Americans cherished the ideals of freedom and individualism, their highest ideal was the democratic principle of majority rule, which he referred to as the "tyranny of the majority". He wrote "I know of no country where there is so little independence of the mind and so little freedom of discussion."

This has had far-reaching consequences on the American psyche. According to cultural analyst David Riesman, author of the renowned study *The Lonely Crowd*, the Americans have become outer-directed people, guided not by their own inner values, but by the opinions of others. Not at all the case for people in "status societies", such as Germany, who feel secure in their niches. Ironically, they accept more eccentric behavior and independent thinking than do Americans, who rely heavily on the approval of the people who surround them.

As the United States is so competitive, the average citizen feels one can only rely on oneself. Such little responsibility to the group has allowed the American to become *homo economicus*, a person directed almost purely by profit-motive, who is supremely mobile and feels almost no family or community obligation.

All this has created a core belief that economic success or misfortune is the individual's responsibility, which, in turn, helps sustain the free-market ideology so popular in the U.S. Supporters of the free-market economy call it "determinist", meaning there are no institutional choices; the market alone decides. Consequently, most Americans believe the destiny of everyone is controlled by profit margins, the global economy, the stock market. Government intervention is frowned upon.

Americans believe that people should be "self-starters", pro-active, not subject to the "herd mentality". One should get things done without any need for external or social pressure. Bill Gates, founder of Microsoft and the richest man in America, symbolizes the image.

The orientation towards results makes people want to excel and be recognized for their accomplishments. The highest aspiration is self-fulfillment and it's only the independent person who can "become" his or her true self. The best indication of how seriously Americans take doing things on their own is the over-use of words like "self-confidence", "self-control", "self-improvement", "self-reliance".

Americans are direct, systematic, action-oriented, and goal-driven. Time is effectively used and saved, not wasted. Americans don't want to wait; they want immediate rewards. It's no accident that fast-food restaurants, like McDonald's, originated in a society that places such emphasis on efficiency.

A phrase one hears frequently in the U.S. is "there's no such thing as a free lunch". Someone who has been born into a rich family and attains success with minimum effort is seen as having had an unfair advantage. High achievement with low effort does not feel right, or make sense, to Americans. Hard work is the key to everything.

The archetypal American is one who starts out as an underdog and becomes a winner, a strong theme in American books and films. The Walt Disney movie *Champions* is one of countless examples. It's the story of a children's hockey team, the Mighty Ducks, which is depicted as hopeless but, through hard work, finishes first in a tournment, the famous "happy ending".

The German need for an enclosed "*Heim*" (home) versus the American "open spaces"

The manner in which a culture deals with space provides us with clues in understanding the psychology of its people. It would be harder to find a greater contrast between Germans and Americans than in their outlook towards room.

Psychologically, Germans feel cramped in their country. Viewed from geographical and demographic perspectives, they are! Germany encompasses 355,744 sq. km., making it slightly larger than the state of New Mexico. Its population is 82 million, or 228 inhabitants per sq. km. In comparison, the United States has 29 inhabitants per sq. km.

Because space is scarce, the Germans have developed a strong attachment to their land and are highly territorial. Heavy population-density means people must conform to more rules, both formal and informal. An example is trying to park a car in a German city. You can be fined 100 Euros should the police (or a passer-by) see you touch another car even if there is no scratch at all as a result.

In Germany, the closed door is the quintessence of order and privacy. It's not because Germans want to do everything in secret, or be left alone and undisturbed. Rather, an open door symbolizes sloppiness and disorganization, provides no protective boundary between people.

It comes as no surprise that Germans place a high value on their homes, which can seem more like vaults than castles. There is a preponderance of fences, walls, hedges and massive doorways; drawn shades keep nosey outsiders from looking in. Sunbathing or talking with friends is always confined to the back yard or balcony.

During World War II, German prisoners of war in the United States displayed their sense of "private sphere". American military authorities housed them in small huts, four to each one. To the astonishment of the Americans, as soon as the prisoners had access to materials, they built partitions. From the American point of view, the scarce materials should have been pooled together to create a larger, more efficient space for the group.

As the home is a refuge from the outside, an invitation to someone's home is something of an honor. Germans compartmentalize their feelings into "public" and "private" selves and don't like to mix the two because it produces a confusion of roles.

In public, a German may seem stiff, overly-rational, even obstinate. In private, the very same person may open up and be extremely friendly and helpful. If an outsider is invited into the private sphere of a German family, it's usually a signal of the possibility of real friendship. In a certain manner, it's a ritual. As everything is regulated in Germany, there are unspoken rules to respect, which include how one chooses one's friends.

Americans are just the opposite when it comes to space. Many observers have remarked that the expansiveness and infinite optimism of the American character are closely linked to geography. Compared to the majority of nations, the size of the United States is overpowering. The distance between Los Angeles and New York is the equivalent of Paris to Moscow, round trip!

Historically, the U.S. has had an excessive amount of land at its disposal: the open frontier. From the 19th until the beginning of the 20th century, Americans were inspired by the motto "Manifest Destiny", which meant they saw themselves as a "chosen people" (justified in expanding their national boundaries all the way to the Pacific). Anyone who felt cramped could pick up stakes and move west. This feeling of open space has had a profound effect on the American perspective. Out on the frontier, you could do almost anything you wanted. There were few people and fewer laws. The result was boundless freedom and universal informality.

The ability to do what one wants is, ironically, governed by a strict code of rules (known as the "rule of law"). Germans, who feel that their country has too many rules and ordinances, are surprised to discover that Americans are obsessive legalists, something confirmed by the excessive number of lawyers and lawsuits in the U.S. In fact, there are four times as many lawyers per capita as there are in Germany. When even a small misunderstanding occurs, the first reaction by an American is often to ask "Do you have a good lawyer?"

In the U.S., houses and apartments are larger, and also cars and roads. Space has not been put to the best of use, at least from a European perspective. Street design in America is treated with incredible casualness. Most left lanes are conceived to be used for turning as well as for through traffic, which causes traffic backups. In Germany — even in the medieval towns where streets are small — planners carefully use all available space and carve out left-turn lanes to ensure a smoother flow of traffic.

Having guests doesn't invade the sense of privacy of Americans, rather it's an extension of their expansiveness. And, as Americans traditionally have a disregard for customs and rules, invitations are of lesser significance than in Germany. They're made more as a convention of conversation (small talk) than as a sincere gesture, something Germans can find quite dismaying. When somebody is actually invited for dinner, the invitation is seldom formal and usually made on short notice ("Are you free tonight?"). Guests are often perceived as temporary members of the family and the host will often tell a hungry guest "just help yourself to the fridge".

The German concept of formal politeness versus the casual American attitude towards etiquette

As mentioned earlier, a leitmotiv that runs through German culture is one of controlling uncertainty. Germans try to avoid mistakes, which explains their conservative dress and proper, often rigid, behavior. This translates into formal politeness,. a kind of built-in respect for others.

Their restrained "correctness" doesn't mean, however, that they're tender with words when criticism must be given. Germans frequently come straight to the point if something is bothering them, even if it means speaking "tactlessly". An example is the pediatric doctor who tells a mother that if she doesn't discipline her over-active two-year-old, the child may well become a juvenile delinquent. The frankness Germans can display shocks people who are used to weighing their words.

Again, this is related to a subconscious fear of uncertainty and a strong desire for clarity. When something goes wrong, they want to get all the facts — good or bad — so that it won't happen again. One sees the same tendency in German journalism. Interviews in *Der Spiegel* or *Stern* get right to the point. If an answer is evasive, the interviewer has no compunction against saying so, often to the surprise and dismay of the interviewee.

Related to the German need to be direct is the way Americans and Germans differ in how they wish to be perceived by others. Americans, for the most part, wish to be liked. Germans want to be seen as credible, to be appreciated as being truthful (*wahrgenommen werden*), especially in working life. Germans tend not to "chit-chat" at cocktail parties. Conversation is made to discuss matters seriously, whether they be important or trivial. If you're not able to do so, you'll be dismissed as a lightweight personality. Germans place more importance on being respected than liked.

Another concept to consider is how politeness in Germany is influenced by the need to compartmentalize. As opposed to the American style of informality, rushing to get on a first-name basis with a German is an absolute taboo. Being too familiar with a person you hardly know is "just not done". Germans want to establish the nature of a relationship before they commit themselves to first names. Private and public/working spheres, as mentioned before, must remain separate.

The language reflects this as well. There are two forms of address for "you", the familiar *du* and the formal *Sie*. *Du* is for family and close friends. *Sie* is always used unless one is invited to do otherwise. It is a code which establishes, yet again, a sense of order. A person can be fined up to 750 Euros for not respecting this rule with civil servants (such as addressing a police officer with the *du* form).

Finally, one shouldn't forget that Germans, as well as most other Europeans, have historically looked to the upper class or old aristocracy as role models in terms of etiquette. Remnants of the class system still emphasize proper manners for anybody who wishes to appear cultured and educated.

America has had a completely different experience when it comes to etiquette. Founded by religious dissenters, peopled by economic refugees, the New World wanted to break away from the constraints of European society. The last thing the various immigrants had on their minds was formality. More urgent things had to be done, namely to build a new existence in a new nation.

This doesn't mean Americans are impolite. They possess a natural courtesy, saying "please" and "thank you" when the circumstances call for it, and are generally respectful towards strangers. Elaborate protocol and formality simply goes against the grain of American democracy. Anybody who acts in a superior or condescending manner is rejected as being a snob. The nation has a strong belief that "all men are created equal". The non-existence of class structure explains why Americans, when writing a letter of complaint, are more likely to address it to the very top, to the president of the company, not the department responsible for the product in question.

American parents raise their children with the notion that constraints or harsh discipline might hurt them psychologically. It is strongly related to their need for upward mobility, which relies heavily on the instruments of praise and/or material rewards. As a result, Americans are generous with flattery and positive feedback. De Tocqueville noted this in his observations: "In dealing with strangers Americans seem to be impatient with the slightest criticism and insatiable for praise."

Having been brought up with few constraints, Americans tend to be direct in an unexacting, casual manner. In fact, they are likely to thoughtlessly "spill the truth" or "let it all hang out". Children may tell their parents "I hate you!" or "you hurt my feelings!" without thinking of the consequences. Later on, as adults, they may tell dinner guests that it's "getting late", an obvious signal for ending an evening. Even if foreigners are taken aback by such directness, American don't mean to be rude.

What has transpired over the years is a national attitude of accepting others as they are, and likewise, being oneself. Americans don't usually have set routines for particular situations, thus don't know their limits. Behavior is usually improvised, an easy-going attitude that's characteristic of a low-context culture. Yet it has its negative side; Americans are sometimes uncertain as to how to behave respectfully towards others.

Recently there has been a movement to define what good manners are, as Americans prominent in business, politics and the professions are aware that they haven't acquired the etiquette tools normally expected. Whether this will change the easy-going attitude towards manners in a land that fiercely protects its individualism remains a question.

The German precise scheduling of time versus the American obsession that "time is money"

Both Germany and the United States are monochronic cultures; they operate according to schedules, one thing at a time. However both cultures conceive of time differently.

The Germans don't think of time in terms of money. Rather, time is to be used to execute activities precisely when they should occur. As many Germans will tell you, the best way to have anarchy is to allow various areas of life to mix. Again, this remark reflects German uneasiness towards uncertainty and ambiguity.

When a decision has to be made, Germans will spend a lot of time and energy to clear things with all parties concerned. Once there is consensus as to a plan, operations will be carried out according to schedule. It is for this reason that the German business pace seems much slower than that in America.

Germans organize time according to work schedules and appointments. In airports and train stations, one always hears *planmäßige Abfahrt* (departure according to plan) over the loudspeakers, a term that emphasizes the planned outcome. They become irritated if something goes awry. This rigid attitude extends to other aspects of life. For example, utility companies will not supply natural gas until November 1 st, even though it might be cold in October.

Interestingly enough, university professors are allowed to be up to 15 minutes late - *das akademische Viertel* - before a lecture is cancelled. Germans use this concept to establish how late is "late" for a business appointment. If a person doesn't call to say he'll be late, the meeting will be called off after the same 15-minute wait.

When invited for dinner, one is expected to arrive on time. This is not to say the Germans are inflexible when it comes to unannounced changes but, in general, being a few minutes late for a dinner engagement or business appointment will be perceived as being inefficient or lacking interest.

The American concept of time finds its roots in Puritan heritage. Useful activities are valuable, meaningful and moral. If one is not actively engaged in meaningful acts, one becomes useless and *immoral*. The American colonist and statesman Benjamin Franklin said: "Do not waste time, it's the stuff life's made of." His thoughts on time have had a profound influence on the American psyche.

To "waste" time is very un-American; to make the hours pass by in idle conversation is considered almost shameful. "He's wasting my time", an often-heard phrase, expresses irritation, if not anger. The only path to success is hard work and, as always, "time is money". Time, like money, can be spent, lost or well invested.

The idea that the present can always be improved upon explains in large part why Americans are always in such a hurry. They want results *now*. Nobody wants to waste time; everything is done as quickly as possible (whether it be negotiations or socializing). This leads to a business culture that features quick decisions, rapid implementation and expectations of completion with minimum delays. The popularity of books such as *The One-Minute Manager* demonstrates how seriously time is treated in the U.S. One constantly looks for ways of doing tasks more efficiently. Finishing sooner saves money and allows more time for leisure activities.

However the American obsession with not wasting time has spilled over into those same leisure activities. If an American sits around the swimming pool too much, he or she gets nervous and feels obliged to do something productive. The famous quotation of an American on holiday, "If it's Tuesday, this must be Belgium," reflects the absurdity of expecting to see seven European countries in a week. In the same vein, quick assembly-line cooking and easy-to-read standard menus, exemplified best by McDonald's, found its roots first in the United States. Everything must be done efficiently and fast, even activities such as traveling and eating.

The German notion of *"Freund"* versus the American idea that everyone is a friend

The Germans are not, by nature, a very outgoing people. Though their daily routine brings them into close contact with many individuals, they are close only to a few. The clear compartmentalization of German social life creates a strong nuance between *Freund* and *Bekannte*. The word *"Freund"* signifies something deep and special, the nearest English equivalent would be "close friend". What Americans refer to as "friends" would be, in German, *gute Bekannte* ("close acquaintances").

Germans take friendship seriously. It means permanence, a protection from the unstable outside world. One often hears the expression *"die Freundschaft pflegen"* (caring for friendship). German friendship tends to be highly selective and profound. It entails long-term commitment and a depth of (unspoken) feeling. Discussions about feelings and the deeper meaning of life are not uncommon. Germans scrupulously separate work and private life to maintain a semblance of order. The same applies to friends and acquaintances.

Friendship is not such a clearly defined notion in the U. S. Visitors are pleasantly surprised by the friendliness Americans display, but many make the mistake of equating friendliness with friendship (and think that they have many new friends). When relationships don't turn out to be what they thought, the complaint is that Americans are superficial and shallow.

What foreigners often fail to understand is that Americans are guided by values of egalitarianism. At the outset, nobody is considered better or worse than anybody else. The all-purpose "Hi" denotes this belief in equality, the message being "I am approachable." It doesn't at all denote a commitment to someone.

As a whole, the term "friend" is less profound than in other cultures. American friendships are marked more by nostagia and sentimentality than by dependence and obligation. As Americans are always on the move — geographically, socially, economically, they've developed strategies to interact superficially with many people. Also, *real* friendship means responsibility and strict bonds of convention (which is diametrically opposed to the American belief in freedom and independence). This may explain why Americans go to psychoanalysts (the actor Woody Allen personifies this in his films) more frequently than Germans. Americans do, however, form sincere, long-term relationships when the situation allows for it.

The German doing something "*gründlich*" and effectively versus the American doing something efficiently with an instant solution

Before discussing these differences, it is important to understand the meaning of the words "effective" and "efficient".

> *Effective means to produce a definite or desired **result**.*
> *Efficient means to produce a desired **effect** with little effort, expense or waste.*

The difference between effectiveness and efficiency can be seen through the interaction of an American-German couple. The German wife mentions one morning that it would be nice to have a shelf in the hallway to store her hats and boxes on. She assumes her American husband will think out the solution thoroughly. The husband, wanting to impress her by getting things done without wasting time, builds the shelf while his wife is out shopping. When she comes back, she's pleasantly surprised by his quick work. She begins putting boxes on it, only to see the shelf come crashing down. Her husband may have been "efficient" but he was far from "effective".

One could say that Germans, as a whole, are driven to be thorough (*gründlich*) and effective, whereas Americans tend to always think about being efficient and fast.

In their book *Taken for a Ride: How Daimler-Benz drove off with Chrysler*, authors Vlasic and Stertz document clearly how Daimler managers effectively outmaneuvered the Chrysler managers. The Germans would think out everything thoroughly with thick binders of data and careful planning, contrasting sharply with the fast, intuitive managment style of the Americans. In the end, the exhaustive planning of the Germans led to their domination of all joint meetings (to the great chagrin of the Americans).

Americans, on the whole, find Germans spend too much time looking for the perfect solution. Americans are ruled by the desire to find a quick fix. They don't feel they have time to doubt. When a problem presents itself, the solution should require minimum effort and expense.

Americans have historically been on the go; they can't stand being held up. They live in the present and future and don't want to be bothered by the past. Time is to be not wasted by asking too many questions or trying to perfect a solution. "Let's get the job done", they say.

When Mercedes-Benz started up its first American car plant in Tuscaloosa, Alabama, the company recruited two top American experts from Ford and General Motors to advise on production. A ferocious dispute occurred when the

German management accused the Americans, in their haste to start production, of wanting to make tin boxes. The Americans responded that the Germans wouldn't ever get anything done if more attention wasn't directed toward production. A classic case of a cultural clash between old craftsmen, who value quality, and production people, who think in terms of results according to a "bottom line".

The German emphasis on "detailed-thinking" versus the American penchant for "non-conventional thinking"

Regardless of the size of a German company, almost everything is directed towards detailed scheduling, consensus-building, and conformity. The probability of failure is reduced to a minimum. German culture is like that of a symphony orchestra, an organization that reflects the dynamics of German society. As in all symphony orchestras, conformity is valued, order is important and the rules are many. Each person is expected to contribute his or her talents for the good of the whole. Essentially, the German sees himself as an integral part of society, and values combined effort.

In German business, management always plans for the long term and in great detail. The following story epitomizes this:

> *Once upon a time, three journalists — a Frenchman, an American and a German — were asked to write a fictional story about the elephant. The Frenchman wrote "L'éléphant et l'amour". The American wrote "Thirty-six Miracle Diets for the Modern Working Elephant". And the German wrote "The Psychological Nature and Fundamental Dynamics of the Socialization of the Elephant: Volume 1, The Symbolic Importance of the Elephant, Chapter 1: From Julius Caesar to the Present".*

This attentiveness, however, usually pays off in higher productivity. An example in contrasts. When the city of Denver opened its new airport in 1995, it had spent 15 months installing the computer-run luggage-handler. On the opening day, the system didn't work. The American company needed another six months to get it running correctly. A similar control-system was installed in a modern shipping center near Leipzig by a German company. It was built in half the time and it functioned perfectly on its first day of operation.

As opposed to the United States, venture capital was practically nonexistent in Germany until the late '90s. Generally, Germans are more reactive than proactive and risk-taking tends to be unpopular. This is not to say that Germans don't take risks, they do. And despite their thoroughness, mistakes can be made. One example is a German car manufacturer's attempt to set up an automobile factory in Pennsylvania in the early '80s. Not having done their intercultural homework, management falsely assumed an American factory worker would possess the same kind of basic training and be as quality-conscious as a German. This was not the case; the quality of manufacturing was poor. In the end, American consumers didn't want to buy the American-made version anymore. The factory was closed, a spectacular failure, costing the company over 500 million Euros.

Americans, by nature, have a "frontier mentality" and continuously seek new challenges. They like and seek people who don't accept conventional thinking and aren't satisfied with the status quo. They can be compared to an American football team, where aggressiveness and individuality are important. The game consists of breaking through lines successively by tactics and force until the goal has been reached, in some ways an extension of the conquering of the Wild West. The players are individualistic but there is also the huddling of the team. Americans are good at getting together to face a problem, working intensely and then scattering.

They value individual creativity very highly. How strongly this runs through the culture is revealed in one of the worst insults an American can give, telling a person he or she is a "total bore".

Another factor explaining why Americans like non-conventional thinking is their suspicion of authority. The U.S. was founded by disregarding and overthrowing the arbitrary rule of King George III of England. This mistrust of authority has remained in the American mindset and laid the foundation for an innovative culture.

After the oil crisis of the early '70s, a group of California cyclists decided to create a safe, easy-riding bike. The American "anything goes" spirit led to the use of exotic materials from the aerospace industry and the creation of a new type of frame combining stability and ruggedness. The "mountain bike" was born, a striking contrast to the racing bikes of classic European design.

The German "*höchste Leistung bringen*" versus the American the "high need to achieve"

This is a difficult contrast to articulate because the differences are subtle, but they are important in how they motivate Germans and Americans. Germans still mostly believe work defines their existence, whereas Americans feel that work determines how well they move up the social ladder, what sort of consumer lifestyle they can have. To understand this, one needs to go deeper by examining the use of the above expressions.

The German expression *höchste Leistung bringen* has no real equivalent in English. Literally, it means "to bring about the highest output or performance", but it is often translated as "to work very intensively". The *Autobahn*, where driving at top speeds is often the norm, is a metaphor of this German need for high performance and passionate intensity.

The glorification of toil and working intensively originates in the Protestant teachings of Martin Luther. He wrote, in the 16th century, that to obtain God's salvation, each individual had a *Berufung* (calling) in life. One's love for God was expressed by performing tasks as well as one could. The frequently-used phrase "*Ich muß meine Pflicht tun*" (I must do my duty) expresses this value. Wasting one's time, taking breaks, doing nothing or enjoying the profit of labor, were all considered sinful. German sociologist Max Weber later called this the "Protestant work ethic".

It continues to influence the working style of Germans (even in the Catholic regions) and is reflected in German expressions such as *Arbeitswut* (work rage). The older generation would fondly say "they lived to work", but this has changed in the last fifteen years. Ironically, of all the nations in Europe, the Germans now work one of the shortest number of hours per year — 1,444 hours per year (*Source: International Labor Organization in Lausanne, Switzerland 2002*). But they still produce the most per capita due to their high intensity.

Many in Germany now complain that Teutonic thoroughness is letting up. This gradual shifting of values, known as *Wertewandel*, was predictable; working hard was the only way out of their collective disaster of 1945. By the early '80s, the country had one of the highest standards of living in the world and Germans began learning how to relax. Despite this change, the German work ethic is still comparatively high.

Many Americans are influenced by the same Protestant work ethic the earlier colonists brought with them. Their intellectual luggage, however, was the system of Calvin rather than of Luther. In it, individuals were predestined to be either chosen for salvation or doomed to condemnation. This led to an existential insecurity and Puritans took refuge in the idea that God's permission to become successful was a sign for being chosen.

This explains largely the roots of the American value the "need to achieve". In a country founded on democratic principles without class distinctions, Americans differentiate themselves through individual material success. Destiny is determined by initiative (being pro-active). The culture demands achievement and once this is demonstrated, a person can participate in the "pursuit of happiness".

This restless "need to achieve" was already described by de Tocqueville:

> *An American will build a house in which to pass his old age and sell it before the roof is on; he will plant a garden and rent it just as the trees are coming into bearing; he will clear a field and leave others to reap the harvest; he will take up a profession and leave it; settle in one place and soon go off.*

Americans are happiest when achievements and success can be documented, measured specifically via scoreboards, bestseller lists, TV ratings, statistics, I.Q.s and, lastly, by their salary. They have an inherent belief in being able to improve just about any aspect of their lives, which explains why they always want to be more efficient, ultimately leading to prosperity. American bookstores mirror this with numerous self-help books (which range from Dale Carnegie's *How to Win Friends and Influence People*, a book on the techniques of becoming popular, to *The Joy of Sex*, a how-to-book on the art of making love). All of them carry the inherent message that one can achieve "happiness" by changing strategies or adopting certain techniques.

German penchant for modesty versus the continual American search for status

German culture has a long tradition of mutual respect among its population. Implicit in this "respect" was that people remained attached to their social class. Life in a "status society" meant a certain modesty and dignity, in that the carpenter was a proud craftsman, the butcher was a skilled meat-cutter, etc. In the last 30 years, however, Germany has gradually changed into a modern consumer society where there is a strong will to improve one's standing. Yet the values of modesty and respect for others have basically remained.

Another point to consider is the envy (*Neid*) factor, which is an essential part of the German psyche. Germany's history — marked by wars, famine and poverty — made it a country where it was often difficult to make a living. When one became rich, it was considered wise and religiously decent (from Luther's teachings of piousness and simplicity) not to show off or provoke envy. Even today, should one become highly successful, people over 40 consider it inappropriate to show off one's wealth. For instance, when affluent Germans buy a Mercedes or BMW, they often ask the dealer to remove the numbers (which refer to the engine size) from the body so that no one can tell how much they paid for the vehicle.

Over the past 150 years, America became home for millions of poor immigrants, mostly from Europe; they came to the New World to start a new existence. The U.S. was created on the ideology of an egalitarian, classless society. This didn't mean people were all the same. Rather, it expressed the idea that everyone had the same right as everyone else to try their luck at a better destiny. On the whole, Americans care less about inequality — the gap between the rich and the poor — than about opportunity and achievement.

As there was no overt class system, the only criterion Americans had to define their standing was what they had measurably accomplished. Status symbols became the visible expression of success. *"Keeping up with the Jones"* (or *"I want what my neighbor has"*) expresses the American ideal of telling the world what one has achieved. Americans commonly talk about their salary, how big their house is or the type of car they drive because they are proud of "making it". Appearance and status, not inner fulfillment or envy, are the basic driving forces of Americans.

The upshot of all this is that *image* in U.S. culture has become more important than *substance*. Americans frequently feel they've achieved something when others see them as "successful". Appearing prosperous is usually enough to convince people that you're an important person.

It can reach absurd levels. A top German consultant — who, himself, commands $450 an hour — says the most important thing for his clients when visiting America is to impress their counterparts. He suggests simply renting a chauffeured limousine at $500 for a day. Americans are convinced your image reflects the quality of your products and ideas.

German concept of *"solide Ausbildung"* versus American preference to "learn by doing"

Back in 1992, the editors of *Newsweek* magazine, in a reaction to the relatively poor educational standards in the United States, undertook a study on which countries did the best job in teaching their young. The editors concluded that the best overall school system to emulate was the German one.

Why? Traditionally, German society has always cherished education. The importance of a *solide Ausbildung* (respectable education and training) is undisputed. In the term *solide Ausbildung*, the word *"solide"* has a deeper meaning than in American English. It implies reliability and character. Schooling that is thorough and dependable is *"solide"*.

This thorough education can be seen in the students who go on to learn a trade at vocational schools. They have much higher academic skills than the counterparts in the U.S.The world-famous *Dualsystem* (working and learning alternatively) is the result of this mentality. Apprentices become excellent and thoroughly-trained workers, the backbone of Germany's economic success. This is often overlooked by American business people and economists. The strong commitment to education and training was demonstrated in 1999 when Daimler-Chrysler put over 6000 workers and managers through a one-year retraining program before they even began to manufacture their new S-class model.

However, the technological computer revolution, along with the global demand for greater cost efficiencies have forced many companies to cut back training, leading one U.S. journalist to write, "The fight for profit is replacing skill and humanity."*

Americans, on the other hand, have always been pragmatic people. To become "cultivated" has never been important and is, in fact, considered elitist. The Declaration of Independence of 1776 states unequivocally that "all men are created equal", which excluded any form of elitism. Americans are fond of saying "If you're so smart, why aren't you rich?"

The U.S. schooling system operates on the theories of the educationalist John Dewey (1859-1952), who stressed that the school's job was to emphasize the natural development of the child rather than force memorization of facts. The child becomes the active agent in his or her own education (rather than the passive receiver of information).

American schools firmly believe in teaching "life skills" — logical thinking, analysis, creative problem-solving. The contents of a given subject are secondary to the actual process. This is the basis of the concept "learn by doing". Learning facts by heart is considered a block to creativity and individuality.

Although there are definite advantages to being an active agent, there is a downside. E.D. Hirsch, in his best-selling book *Cultural Literacy*, points out that students who have not acquired a solid base in facts and background information will have difficulty expressing themselves, be it in writing or verbally. The book had a profound effect on the U.S. educational system in the mid-'90s. Schools have now begun returning to methods of rote memorization and giving more homework.

As everything is geared to the short and practical, training is done quickly in the U.S., the "learn by doing" approach. "Jack-of-all-trades" is a popular term, reflecting the strong belief that a person can do anything and everything.

---

*) See Epilogue, pg. 89 for a more detailed explanation

One area where American education excels is at the university and graduate school level. Here, intelligent inquiry and a tradition of "non-conventional" thinking pays off in producing original ideas and innovative products.

Summary of Psychological Characteristics

Germans tend to be	**Americans tend to be**
— serious	— overly self-confident
— afraid of uncertainty	— optimistic
— neat and orderly	— overly familiar and casual
— perfectionists	— improvisers
— conservative in manner	— expansive
— formal	— informal
— loath to take risks	— risk takers
— meticulous about schedules	— driven by "time is money"
— selective in friendship	— friendly to everyone
— group oriented	— individualists
— effective & thorough in work	— efficient & fast in work
— detail-oriented	— non-conventional-oriented
— intense about their work	— obsessed with a need to achieve
— modest	— image-oriented
— generally well-trained	— sometimes lacking in basic training

Discussion Questions

1. Do you think there are other factors, apart from war, that have influenced the Germans to be orderly and serious?

2. What are the long-term consequences of the American "inner separation" from others (as pointed by Alan Roland) on their behavior in business?

3. Do you believe that Germans can adopt the American philosophy "the pursuit of happiness"?

4. With one of the highest standards of living in the world, do you think Germans might become less concerned about perfection and the need for order?

Chapter 3

Cultural Differences in the American and German Business Worlds

Can't anybody work overtime?

Paul Wilson, the new American manager at Schulz Metallfabrik, was looking at sales reports when the administrative assistant came into the office and closed the door. "Herr Wilson, we have just received a large order from an automobile plant in Great Britain. Our problem is the delivery date. The company wants everything by the end of the month. That means we have only seven days to complete it and we're already booked up with other orders."

Wilson looked somewhat surprised and said, "I don't see where the problem is. Tell everybody we'll be working overtime, including this weekend. We'll start today."

His assistant seemed baffled, then blurted out: "Herr Wilson, you can't make a last-minute request for overtime just like that. German employees are protected from arbitrary decisions of management. We have to get permission from the Betriebsrat *first!"*

The American expatriate asked himself why Germans were so hung-up about getting permission to work overtime? Workers usually like overtime because of the extra money. And anyway, he thought, you can't refuse a rush-order. If Germans didn't change their ways, the company would start losing money.

Both the American and German business worlds are characterized as being goal-oriented, giving great importance to individual performance, perseverance and hard work. But the manner the two cultures go about achieving these things are quite different, as the following comparisons will show.

German task-oriented style versus the American need to be result-oriented

The one dominant characteristic of the German worker is a fixation to accomplish tasks. Traditionally, work is divided into well-defined parts and a person is designated a job to fulfill. A German worker says *"Ich habe einen Auftrag*

43

erhalten" (I have received a task). The emphasis is on completing it and producing quality, no less, no more.

In general, Germans react to problems, they don't seek them out. They like complicated challenges, however, and are good at finding complex solutions. Some of the world's most influential inventors and organizers are Germans, such as Gottlieb Daimler, the inventor of the automobile. Or Wernher von Braun, the brilliant rocket researcher, who was taken by the American armed forces after World War II and put in charge of the American space program. He made it into a highly effective operation, to become known as NASA, that eventually landed the first man on the moon.

Americans are motivated by results and making money. A worker focuses on what can be done within a particular time-frame. Americans prefer to make quick decisions. The importance on tangible goals goes hand in hand with the nation's immigrant history and the driving mantra of "upward mobility". It is for this reason American children are encouraged to take the initiative in life, moving forward into the unknown.

In all activities Americans undertake, the emphasis is not only to finish the task but also to go on to the next level. The superstar Michael Jordan not only became the greatest player in the history of basketball, he created his own style of clothing, sporting goods equipment and even starred in a satirical film about himself.

The strong partnership of business and government in Germany versus their uneasy relationship in the U.S.

The German economy is based on consensus and cooperation. Its main principle is that of the "social pact", an association of labor, business and government, based on the common-sense idea of partnership. Instead of emphasizing adversarial positions that lead to recurrent labor confrontations, government, unions and management look for compromises to assure long periods of industrial peace and employment. This attitude of cooperation is exemplified by the *Mitbestimmungsrecht* (the right to participate), which brings the unions into the corporate decision-making process.

Consensus has had a long tradition in Germany. Otto von Bismarck introduced medical and pension insurance for all workers in 1871. In 1948, Economics Minister Ludwig Erhard launched the *Soziale Marktwirtschaft*, which combined the principles of a free-market economy with an extensive social security program.

Partnership between government and business is exemplified by the large holdings that federal and state governments have in hundreds of companies. For example, the State of Lower Saxony has almost a 20% share of Volkswagen AG. In addition, government subsidies, usually in the form of credit guarantees, help companies export. German companies and contractors can receive up to 100% guarantees in high-risk ventures, making them very competitive in the global marketplace.

This long tradition of maintaining consensus is starting to be questioned, however. With the advent of globalization and the fact many large German companies have adopted the American system of stock-options and bonuses, it remains to be seen if industry, labor and government can maintain their social consensus.*

Americans traditionally view government with distrust. Political interference goes against the nature of being self-supporting and independent. A favorite quote is "All power corrupts and absolute power corrupts absolutely". This suspicion toward government was remarked by de Tocqueville: "An American attends to his private affairs as if he were alone in the world."

The aversion toward government is reflected in the non-socialistic character of American business. According to a study done by the International Monetary Fund in the '80s, more than 95% of the U.S. economy is run by private companies. Practically all telecommunications (including television and radio), energy, transportation and health care systems are in private hands.

Unlike most other industrial democracies, the federal government doesn't promote active partnership with business, but rather an unofficial one. American business is extremely active in Washington via its lobbies, exerting influence over government policy. At the same time, it suggests that government keep bureaucracy at a distance. Although there is no direct relationship between business and government, there are indirect subsidies. For example, Boeing's research and development is heavily financed via military contracts with the Pentagon.

State and local governments have a more direct impact on business. In order to attract companies to their areas, state and municipal officials are usually willing to waive fees and taxes for up to five years in a row. Alabama's generous tax breaks and subsidies were the main reasons Mercedes-Benz established a plant in Tuscaloosa.

German in-house development of managers versus American "hired guns"

German companies, on the whole, seek stability and think in the long term,

---

) See Epilogue, pg. 89 for a more detailed explanation.

which has a direct effect on how they handle their employees. Because management's outlook is conservative, they don't practice destabilizing policies such as "hire and fire" (German labor law is such that it is, in fact, extremely difficult to fire people). They prefer to provide security to their personnel and, in return, expect loyalty from them. Consequently, it's more likely that an employee within the company will rise to become a manager.

Studies show that if job-hopping does occur, it's more likely to happen between foreign-owned companies than family-owned ones. In fact, Germans are generally conservative when it comes to moving for professional reasons; they'd rather stay in their hometowns, even if it means passing up a promotion and better pay.

Moving up the corporate ladder on the fast track is rare. Likewise, taking the initiative as a shortcut to promotion, frequently the case in the U.S., is not considered the best way to rise. More important are training, qualifications and experience. Promotion in Germany is based on planned progression.

Americans still retain the "frontier mentality" that pushes a person to continuously seek new adventures and challenges. The high value placed on individualism and self-assertion means people seldom identify with a group. The American *homo economicus* is more concerned with career and wealth than with loyalty to company or friends.

The word loyalty has a significantly different meaning in American culture. The following account, told by a German manager working for his subsidiary in New York, illustrates the kind of cross-cultural misinterpretation that can occur with a concept.

> *The top American assistant informed his manager that he'd found a better opportunity and would soon be leaving. He said, "I've liked working for this company. To show my loyalty, I'll stay on for the next two weeks." The German manager was stunned. He pointed out that if a German were leaving his company and wanted to show his loyalty, he'd give up to six months' notice.*

How can we interpret this? When a better opportunity presents itself, Americans have absolutely no scruples in jumping to another firm that offers a better deal and conditions. An American executive summed it up this way: "For the most part, Americans regard their company objectively, as a vehicle by which one gains power, self-satisfaction, professional stimuli and income. It is a means to an end."

The lack of working flexibility among Germans versus the American "can do" mentality

German society seeks order and the business world mirrors this with strongly established roles for all employees. Responsibility is clearly defined in the job description. Once workers know their duties, they literally close themselves off from anything that goes beyond their designated position. When workers are asked to perform extra services, they usually say "*Ich bin nicht dafür zuständig*" (I am not responsible for that). This rigidity is the extension of a society where people are generally content with their class status. As opposed to Americans, Germans feel secure knowing their place in the social order. And, once in a specific job, it is extremely difficult to get into a new field of business.

It should be pointed out, however, that with the pressures of globalization and the Internet revolution, many, especially of the younger generation, are questioning these values. Companies in new branches — such as computers, multi-media, and advertising — are adopting values of speed, flexibility and efficiency, so commonly identified with U. S. firms.

Finally, closed office doors underline the message of extreme compartmentalization. Most Germans feel uncomfortable with the "open-office" principle so prevalent in American companies. The territorial attitude of the German worker means he or she is unlikely to share information with people outside the department. Lack of information-flow is a great handicap for Germans in business.

Americans are taught not to recognize their places in society and are constantly asserting themselves. They are programmed to improve their situation. Even if they're not qualified for a desired position, they'll say they are, figuring they'll learn what they have to "on the job".

The upshot of this is a nation open to fast-talking operators. Boasting about one's supposed talents goes a long way in a country with a "can do" attitude. The most flagrant example of this was Ronald Reagan, a highly-talented and persuasive speaker. He started out as a radio announcer, went to Hollywood to become a movie star, then leaped into politics, becoming governor of California before moving on to the White House for eight years.

The modest image of German business versus "the business of America is business"

Americans transferred to Germany are surprised to learn that business doesn't enjoy the same status there as it does in the U.S. Despite enjoying the highest standard of living in Europe, due in part to the success of industry and the partnership between labor and industry, the German worker and general population still view business with reticence.

There are many reasons. Germany had a long history of class exploitation, which reached its peak after World War I when monopolies ruled both economically and politically. This turned a lot of Germans into socialists, and even communists.

It's no accident that the great social critic of the 19th century, Karl Marx, came from Germany. His favorite expression *Ausbeutung* (exploitation) is more frequently used in Europe than in America. Workers are more sensitive to this concept and, through the power of the unions, they have been able to obtain a more equal distribution of wealth than in the United States.

German businesses, until recently, had little understanding of public relations. A vivid example is that of Daimler-Benz. Until 1987, it had no unified corporate image. Company management didn't feel the necessity to tell the public about itself. This laissez-faire attitude toward the public has changed considerably in the past ten years with far more public relations campaigns by German companies.

"The business of America is business" is a famous 1920s quotation expressing the collective feeling Americans had toward business. By and large, business still enjoys a very good reputation in the U.S. The explanation is simple.

American culture is commonly thought to begin with the first English settlement in 1607. The country's economic progress since has been phenomenal: from wilderness to computer technology in less then four centuries. Endless natural resources allowed the United States to create a society of abundance, helped along by wave after wave of immigrants who never stopped looking for ways to improve things.

The personal wealth Americans have attained isn't thought of as having been gained at the expense of others. The average American believes that the dynamic nature of business creates opportunities and jobs for others. As opposed to German culture, where success is often viewed with *Neid* (envy), most Americans admire successful and wealthy people. They hope to become rich themselves!

German need for a business "relationship" versus American strict adherence to the contract

Germans, like most continental Europeans, have traditionally viewed a business deal as the building of a personal relationship. An agreement is often verbal and signed with a handshake. It's based on the premise of *Vertrauen gegen Vertrauen* (trust begets trust). [The author worked 16 years on a free-lance basis for Daimler-Benz and never once signed a contract. Everything was agreed upon orally.]

Of course, most deals in Germany do involve signed contracts, but they're still geared toward long-term relationships rather than short-term objectives. A spirt of compromise between parties, a "win-win" situation is seen as simple common sense. And the written contracts usually don't contain clauses covering every possible situation which might arise (usually the case in America). If a conflict occurs, the courts will interpret the contract in the *Treu und Glaube* (good faith) tradition. This means that, within its framework, a logical structure can be found and carried over to a new situation.

For Americans, the contract is perceived as a sacred document. The phrase *"A deal is a deal"* is often heard, meaning the contract can't be changed or broken. Inductive in nature (see page 60), it will specify in fine detail all the important points and usually even contain a number of *possibility clauses.* Should one party dare not respect one clause, the other party won't hesitate to go to court and sue for damages. The emphasis is on immediate results and profits, not the continuing relationship.

This fastidious enforcement of "fine print" is strongly related to the American belief in equality. In order to make sure these ideals are enforced, social behavior has been codified into strict rules and laws. "In America, all classes show great respect for the law," wrote de Tocqueville in 1835. This is why there are so many lawyers in the U.S.: they're needed to interpret how one should behave in a society that originally had no tradition to fall back on.

Discrimination toward women in German business versus American "equality of the sexes"

Historically, German women were delegated to the traditional role of a devoted wife and mother, based on the old *Kinder, Küche, Kirche* (children, kitchen, church) ideology. Despite changes in the Civil Code in the '60s and '70s (that gave German women the right to own property and protected that property in case of divorce), women have difficulty in attaining executive positions in the business world. Compared to other industrialized nations, the "glass ceiling" (the elusive barrier within a company hierarchy that prevents women from obtaining upper-level positions) is extremely low. A 1963 survey found that only 3.4 percent of West

German executives were female. A similar survey carried out by the German government in 2002 found that only 4.3 percent of top managers were women.

German society doesn't encourage women to strive for top positions, especially if they want to have children. Daycare centers are still rare. School normally ends at noon or 1 p.m., making it difficult to take up a high-power career and to be a satisfactory mother at the same time. There are also salary disparities, with women earning only about 70% of what men do. On the other hand, not all avenues are closed to German women. In the *Bundestag*, roughly ten percent of the members are women.

American women, in general, have more of a chance to move up the corporate ladder. They are also more visible. In 1992, 16% of all leading executive positions were filled by women. One reason is that the U.S. Congress passed strict laws concerning equal rights. Companies that don't promote women (or that tolerate sexual harassment in the workplace) can be sued. The "help wanted" ads in newspapers are not allowed to describe jobs on the basis of gender. A growing number of American women are putting off marriage and/or motherhood to further their careers. This has given way to the perception that American women are on the top of the world.

But recent studies show no matter how bright a woman is, she is still not taken as seriously as a man. In other words, a woman has to work harder to attain an executive position. Despite all the legal advances, women normally work longer hours than men and salary differences between men and women are approximately the same as in Germany.

With the increased number of women in the corporate world, many commentators thought that "female values" would make their presence felt: business would become less competitive and more concerned with human issues. That doesn't seem to have happened. Instead, women have mostly fashioned themselves to fit into the "man's world".

The Concept of German and American Managers:
A Clash in Perception

American business schools are proud of their management theories and feel they are universally applicable. However, American-style management may not apply outside the borders of the U.S. As we shall see, the term "manager" has a very different meaning in Germany.

The linguistic origin of the word "manage" comes from the Latin *manus,* meaning hand. Later, in Italian, it was transformed into *maneggiare,* which is the training of horses in the *manege*; subsequently, its meaning became skillful handling in general. The French transformed it to *ménage,* the art of running a household. Today "to manage" means to direct or administer.

What is a manager in the American cultural context? The roots are to be found in the writings of Adam Smith, author of the 1776 book *The Wealth of Nations* as well as those of the 19th century British economist John Stuart Mill. In his 1911 work, *The Principles of Scientific Management,* social scientist Frederick Taylor defined managers as a class of people that: (1) do not own a business but sell their skills on behalf of the owners, and (2) do not produce personally but are indispensable in making others produce (through "motivation").

Although the core element of a work organization is the people who do the work, American business has stressed that the individual manager is the key to success. Up until the Enron and WorldCom scandals, managers were considered by many to be heroes. When Walt Disney CEO Michael Eisner made $575 million in 1997, he was treated like a "rock star" in the media.

But managers derive their *raison d'être* from the people managed. A manager is part of the group he or she leads. Japanese and, to a lesser extent, European businesses follow this line; the labor force participates in decisions, guided by the manager.

A reason why the managerial class is looked upon as the core of U.S. enterprise is the relative lack of skilled workers in North America, something that can be traced back to the Industrial Revolution. Economic historian Alfred Chandler points out in his book, *Scale and Scope — The Dynamics of Industrial Capitalism,* that the process of industrialization in the U.S. and Europe was quite different. Whereas America possessed enormous natural resources and land, skilled workers were a rarity. Europe, on the other hand, had well-trained workers but lacked raw materials.

These two distinct starting points have had long-term consequences, with the U.S. favoring standardized and time-saving production processes (Taylorism), which allowed unskilled workers, who were not expected to participate in decisions, to be hired. In Europe, mid-sized industries grew through the flexible use of skilled workers who, along with management, made production innovation.

Another reason for the high regard managers have in the U.S. is, once again, traditional distrust of collective authority. There exists no national training program to produce skilled craftsmen. What has transpired is a semi-skilled workforce that is able to do passable work at various trades. (It is interesting to note that the expression "jack-of-all-trades" is a frequently used term in America, while its near equivalent in German — *Hansdampf in allen Gassen* — is rarely heard.)

It has been a leitmotiv of American culture that anybody with two hands can "learn on the job". Workers are often quickly trained and quality control and motivation are the manager's responsibility.

How does German management differ from American management? International experts agree that one of the greatest assets the German economy possesses is the aforementioned *Dualsystem*, in which young people are thoroughly trained for the working world (whether it be in the office or on the shop floor). Its success goes back to the medieval guild system, which emphasized skilled craftsmen. Training alternates practical work with classroom courses. At the end of the apprenticeship, usually three years, the worker receives a *Facharbeiterbrief*. This certificate is highly valued and instills a sense of occupational pride. Quite a few German company presidents began their careers as apprentices. The present CEO of Daimler-Chrysler, Jürgen Schrempp, started out as an auto mechanic.

Studies done in similar British and French companies show that Germany has the highest percentage of personnel in productive roles and the lowest both in leadership and staff roles. This is directly related to the German apprenticeship program.

Because they are trained to be responsible, German workers expect their boss, or *Meister*, to assign tasks. In turn, they solve the technical problems themselves, a challenge to their acquired skills. That some person has to emotionally "motivate" them would be seen as unnecessary hand-holding and an insult to their professional pride.

The same level of pride is often lacking in the U.S. The author had the experience of dealing with German mechanics who'd been sent to help American Mercedes dealers improve their repair services. All of them reported continual astonishment at the poor general education and overall lack of qualifications exhibited by U.S. mechanics.

> *One young Meister mechanic commented on how he shocked the owner of a North Carolina dealership by figuring out how much diesel fuel was left in a boat's fuel tank without the aid of a fuel gauge. He sank a dipstick into the tank and extrapolated how many gallons were left by calculating the fuel tank's volume. The American owner looked at him as if he were a genius.*

It is interesting to note that, back in 1973, the U. S. consulting firm of Booz, Allen, and Hamilton was commissioned by the German Ministry of Economic Affairs to write a study of German management from an American viewpoint. The cultural bias of the consultants was obvious when they wrote "Germans simply do not have a very strong concept of management". They came to this conclusion, despite Germany's strong economic performance, because German managers and executives have traditionally been educated as technical experts, not MBAs. Over 60% of German manufacturing companies are run by engineers with Ph.D.s. If any management skills had been learned, it was in an improvised manner on the shop floor.

The consulting firm also failed to consider the importance of perfectionism in German culture, where people are automatically expected to strive for the very best in themselves and in others. Workers are likely to say *"Machen wir es richtig"* (let's do it right). Managers don't see any reason to learn about motivating and or even supervising personnel; they assume the work will be done well without any prodding. Detailed information is provided about everything involved. Procedures are to be orderly and followed faithfully. If there is a problem, the employee is expected to solve it.

Historian Paul Kennedy, in his book *The Rise and Fall of the Great Powers,* mentions how the relative independence and thorough training of German employees can affect history. According to Kennedy, a major reason why the German army was able to hold out for so long during World War II (despite the overwhelming superiority of the Allied forces) was the extraordinarily high caliber and training of both the staff officers and the NCOs. Their thorough preparation allowed the German army to implement an operational doctrine, known as the *"Inneren Führung"* principle, that "emphasized flexibility and decentralized decision-making at the *battlefield* level, which proved far superior to the enthusiastic but unprofessional forward rushes of the American forces."

As opposed to Americans, German managers rarely compliment someone on a job well done. The following story illustrates this:

> *An American executive, after working one year for a German company, increased the sales of his department by 45%. Meeting with his bosses, he asked how he was doing. "We haven't had any complaints" was the answer. The American was shocked, but later understood that "an American boss criticizes by not praising and a German boss praises by not criticizing".*

Likewise, if there is a foul up, the manager tends to believe the problem is to be found in a badly-conceived system, not in the employee. The German manager is more concerned with maintaining institutional control and procedures than individual control within a department.

On a final note, it is interesting to consider whether American theories on management have dealt sufficiently with the issue of work as a collective phenomenon. As globalization becomes a force to be reckoned with, it's becoming clear that individual solutions are not necessarily the best. A better concept of management can perhaps be found in consensus-oriented organizations, coupled with a German-style *"Dualsystem"*.

Motivation — How do Germans and Americans differ?

To understand motivation within a culture, one needs to look at basic social assumptions and values. Geert Hofstede examined the masculinity / femininity dimension in societies to see how reward and need-fulfillment could effect motivation.

He found that if a culture was masculine, motivation was translated into money, titles, or other materialistic or status-oriented rewards. In a feminine society, meaningful goals were time off, improved benefits or symbolic rewards. With that in mind, let us re-examine American and German basic assumptions.

Basic Assumptions in American Society

The U.S. is a masculine society with a pro-active and optimistic approach to life. Americans see themselves as ambitious, hardworking, innovative and energetic. Deeply embedded in their psyche is the notion of "pulling yourself up by the bootstraps". Success depends only on how badly you want it; "the sky's the limit". Hard work, honesty and perseverance guarantee rewards.

As before, Americans are fairly obsessed with "individual freedom", which makes them self-starters. Team spirit exists but only when necessary. Fatalism is rare because it is assumed that one controls one's destiny. Competition is a core value among Americans, leading to improvement and growth.

On the negative side, the competitive drive leads to excesses: "winning is everything", "going for the jugular", "he's a loser" or "we don't take prisoners". Because Americans see themselves as individuals, they are more loyal to their own career aspirations than the goals of the company they work for.

Basic Assumptions in German Society

Germans form a masculine society with feminine undertones. Like Americans, they are competitive and ambitious. At the same time, as mentioned before, they want to work collectively and keep to a plan. Government, industry and unions collaborate to establish policies of "mutual benefit" and the system is referred to as a *Soziale Marktwirtschaft* (social-market economy).

German fear of uncertainty puts pressure on employees to strive for *Kollegialität* (collegiality) and display dislike for non-conformist behavior. The end result is consensus and a sense of group welfare. Salary is important, but quality of life and working relationships count a great deal. As they are more loyal to the company, German workers expect more entitlements, such as six weeks' vacation and *Kururlaub* (health spa holiday).

The different values on motivation affect employee compensation in Germany and America. For example, DaimlerChrysler's biggest problem after the merger was trying to harmonize pay structures. According to a Chrysler study in 1998, the average German worker earned $11.40 more per hour than his American counterpart, or $20,000 more annually. With its 200,000 wage-earners, the cost to Daimler was a tidy $4 billion a year.

The higher costs reflect the German culture of social consensus and work in partnership, a feminine characteristic. But the costlier pay-scale can also be considered long-term strategy; it helps maintain morale (there are rarely any strikes), creates loyalty and a sense of duty among employees and results in high quality work.

In the spirit of free-wheeling American capitalism, managers' salaries exhibit the "winner take all" attitude. The obsession to make as much money as possible was already noted by de Tocqueville: "I know no other country where love of money has such a grip on men's hearts or where stronger scorn is expressed for the theory of permanent equality of property." Despite the fact that both companies had approximately the same sales turnover, Chrysler CEO Robert Eaton made eight times more money than Jürgen Schrempp of Daimler at the time of the merger. Likewise, managers in Detroit earned approximately twice as much as German ones.

American culture tends to take the point of view that sharing profits with workers is a "socialist" (some might even say "communist") idea. In the U.S., relations are usually adversarial and aimed at short-term gain. The American-German culture clash is that of individualism versus egalitarianism.

<u>Summary of Cultural Differences in the Business World</u>

Germans tend to be	**Americans tend to be**
— task-oriented	— result-oriented
— reactive	— pro-active
— long-term oriented	— short-term oriented
— pro-government	— anti-government
— loyal to the company	— loyal to themselves
— secure in a well-defined position	— always looking for a better position
— more reserved towards business	— pro-business
— relationship-oriented in contracts	— short-term deal oriented in contracts
— discriminatory toward female employees	— more aware of female employees' rights
— highly-skilled	— not always well-trained
— quality-of-life oriented	— materialistic
— accepting of collective authority	— distrustful of collective authority
— consensus-oriented	— competitive and individualistic
— masculine with feminine overtones	— masculine

Discussion Questions

1. Do you think globalization will lead to less partnership between government, business and labor in Germany?

2. What are the advantages and disadvantages of job hopping from company to company?

3. Why do you think that — despite high wages, a lack of flexibility, compartmentalization — Germany is still the leading exporter per capita in the world?

4. Will there ever be a day when women will be equally present in senior executive positions?

5. In this day and age of increasing computerized automation, is there still a need for the *"Dualsystem"*?

6. What are your views on costlier pay-scale for German workers versus high salaries for American executives?

Chapter 4

Business Meetings

A Detailed Beginning of a German Meeting

Bob Young had just arrived in Frankfurt from Boston. A chauffeured limousine was waiting to drive him to the Hühn & Wein company hideaway. This was his first time in Germany and Bob was looking forward to meeting his new partners. Upon arriving, he found a mixed group of German and Dutch executives waiting. A young woman came in and introduced herself as the chair. To Bob's surprise, she didn't ask the group to introduce themselves but walked to the flip-chart.

She proceeded to read the time schedule. "The meeting begins at 9 o'clock. At 10:15 we'll have our first coffee break, which will last 15 minutes. At 12 we'll go off to lunch. At 12:50 a walk around the park is planned, which will last about one hour. At 2 the meeting will continue. At 3:15, another 15-minute coffee break. The meeting finishes at 4:30." After this military-like description, she asked the participants to introduce themselves. Bob concluded that Germans were more interested in planning than people.

In many respects, American and German behavior is similar in meetings — they communicate in a direct and low-context fashion. But again, there are some major differences in how the two groups operate.

The Americans
Eagerness to get results

The one characteristic that sets Americans apart from other nationalities is their obsession with getting results, i.e. making money fast. "Time is money", "let's wheel and deal", "we don't care what you do or how you do it as long as it gets done", "time-management" and "what's the bottom line?" are all popular expressions.

Americans want to get down to business as quickly as possible. They have little inclination to get to know the other person. A typical attitude is "Why fool around chit-chatting when we could be making deals?" This reflects itself in tightly-framed meetings with set time-limits, designed to obtain rapid agreements. Generally, Americans don't want to think in complex terms or discuss hypothetical situations, as it holds up the pace.

Because they're perpetually in a hurry, they squeeze every minute they can into their working day. This has given rise to the "power breakfast" meeting. For the non-initiated, the purpose of a business breakfast is not to take your first meal of the day, but to conduct business within a 45-minute period.

Inductive Thinking

American thought processes are by nature inductive, making first empirical observations, then collectioning and analysing data, to finally derive principles. This pattern of thought has been characterized as procedural thinking, in which a sequence of individual points are focused on and solved before moving on to the bigger picture.

Being restless in nature, Americans like to claim that "progress" has been made when a few points have been agreed upon. This can be quite confusing for Germans, who are deductive in nature. They don't think it makes any sense to discuss the individual points until there is a "mutual understanding" of the complete situation.

Informality

Parallel to getting straight to the point is the generally informal atmosphere that prevails. Americans like informality because it speeds things up and makes the participants feel at ease. A reserved attitude may be interpreted as being aloof or pretentious. This explains, in part, why Americans are good at forming quick, disposable relationships. Typically, you'll hear "Let's not waste time on formalities. My name's Bob. What's yours?"

The American desire for "egalitarianism" is also at work here. Historically, there has been relatively little importance attached to titles. Nothing will make an American angrier than arbitrary ranking of class. American managers will go out of their way to display camaraderie with their subordinates. In an effort to appear like "one of the gang" the manager might put his feet on his desk and invite everyone to call him by his first name. Despite this display, everyone is well aware who is in command.

Improvised Thinking

To be creative is highly prized in American culture, which goes hand in hand with the belief that innovation increases efficiency (and makes everyone more prosperous).

American meetings are tightly organized. But when a solution must be found quickly, participants will come up with one idea after another in a disorganized and impulsive manner, expecting others to react with instantaneous feedback. This is known as brainstorming. Managers expect ideas from subordinates and subordinates may freely contradict the boss (within reason). Americans are excellent at such exercises because they've been trained to challenge hierarchy and the status quo.

Germans, as a whole, feel uncomfortable with this method, as it doesn't necessarily provide a thorough understanding of a problem. They view it as "thoughtless actionism".

Winning is everything

The world of sports exerts a great influence on the American attitude toward negotiations. Upon closer examination of American sporting events, you find that ending with a tie score goes against the American mindset. What businesspeople subconsciously strive for is what legendary football coach Vince Lombardi kept saying to his team: "Winning isn't everything. It's the only thing."

You can tell a lot about the priorities of a nation by the metaphors they use the most. In the U.S., it is the baseball metaphors and phrases that have found themselves in business vocabulary. When negotiating, American businesspeople like to "play hardball", "to be on a winning streak"; an estimate is a "ball-park figure", they play "winner take all" and (a military term) "take no prisoners". As opposed to Germans, Americans often have trouble compromising in business deals. "Compromise is okay," they say, as long as the other guy compromises more than you.

In recent years a new philosophy has come into vogue, namely the "win-win" strategy. Both parties in a negotiation must come out as winners. Astute businesspeople know that this is the best policy in the long run.

The Poker Face

Foreigners can easily be fooled by the American negotiating style, which is characterized as open and straightforward. Beneath the facade, there is an intense drive to win. It is said that most successful negotiators are excellent poker players. "To keep a poker face" and "never let them see you sweat" are indicative of how the American negotiator works. It's always important to maintain a cool, balanced posture.

A sudden outburst of anger on the part of the American is more than likely to be showmanship, meant to gain a psychological advantage. As American business culture is strongly influenced by Puritan values, negotiators rarely resort to false statements. (This doesn't mean to say they won't use selective data to support a point.)

To throw off their opponents, some start with exaggerated demands, then give up "substantial interests" which are often unimportant. This was a favorite technique of President Reagan when trying to get a piece of legislation passed in the U.S. Congress. He'd make many (in reality, minor) concessions and say he'd "gone the extra mile".

The Germans

Importance of Extensive Background Information

Before any agreement is reached, Germans want to be *sure* they have all the relevant facts. They tend to look to historical precedents to understand the present. Thus, an introductory speech will include a lot of background information, giving a perspective many Americans would leave out.

Presentations can be long (up to an hour), but Germans are conditioned to this and are patient listeners. The tendency to be excessively analytical and complex may be perceived by Americans as over-doing it, a sort of "paralysis through analysis".

Like Americans, Germans expect visuals and lots of figures to illustrate the points being made. The difference is that they tend to provide more information than most Americans think they need. Former Chrysler CEO Robert Eaton, after his first meeting with members of the Daimler-Benz Board, summarized this by saying, "The Germans have a penchant for coming to all meetings armed with tons of overhead transparencies and colored charts. It's information overkill."

Deductive Thinking

Unlike Americans, Germans think more in a deductive manner, reasoning from a known, general principle to the specific, logical conclusion. They will state the nature of a problem, from which a systematic analysis of goals, conditions and past experience will lead to an examination of all options. After careful consideration of all the choices, the best option is chosen. The Germans strive for a complete and logically-constructed argument so that the conclusion is virtually unavoidable.

This accounts for the fact that Germans often have a tendency to speak in long monologues. To build up a logically thought-out idea, it takes time. It is not advisable to interrupt a German who is trying to create a coherent argument. Disturbing his train of thoughts will throw him off balance and can provoke mistrust and anger.

Formalism

The Germans perceive themselves as being polite and expect visitors to behave accordingly. The American manner of getting to know their counterparts by saying "just call me Joe" isn't accepted by Germans who have a strong sense of privacy. What it comes down to is that Germans feel uncomfortable with what they perceive as "promiscuous familiarity".

Protocol dictates that the first thing to do at a meeting is to shake hands all around. As Germans respect hierarchy, the highest-ranking visitor is expected to introduce himself or herself. The other members of the team introduce themselves by seniority. Each person gives a brief description of their area of responsibility. Then the hosts introduce themselves in turn.

During a break, Germans don't normally "shoot the breeze" (an expression which has no equivalent in the German language). Life is seen as too serious to waste time on nonsense. When non-business subjects are discussed, even trivial matters like sports or vacation plans, it is done in an earnest tone.

Understated Salesmanship

Germans are determined to make sure that they do things correctly and want only solid information. Wild Hollywood-like gesticulation and hard-sell talk won't go down well. Also, jokes and humor are considered to be distractions, not helpful.

Cartoon-style images on charts and graphs don't mix with business in the German mind. Likewise, attacking your competitors' products is not the way Germans operate. In their minds, a product or idea that is good will stand on its own merits. There's no need to put down the competitor.

A Wariness of Immediate Results

Germans are not obsessed with quick results. Although it may exasperate Americans, their strategy is, as previously mentioned, to think in the long term without worrying too much about immediate returns.

Their habit of carefully weighing alternatives makes them seem reticent. One astute observer described the approach as "systematically pragmatic". Although

Germans can be good participants in brainstorming sessions, their real nature is that of being analytical and objective (*sachlich*). (*A detailed explanation of this can be found in Appendix C, pg. 108*).

Summary of American-German Business Meetings

Germans tend to be	Americans tend to be
— formal	— informal
— deductive	— inductive
— systematic	— improvised thinkers
— slower in decision-making	— eager to get immediate results
— insistent on extensive information	— satisfied with minimum information

Discussion Questions

1. What societal values explain the American eagerness to get results?

2. Do you think the German wariness toward immediate results leads to missed business opportunities?

3. In negotiating with someone from another culture, which recommendations do you think would be useful for you? Why? Can you think of other tips to give those preparing for cross-cultural negotiations?

Chapter 5

Language and Communication

The myth that America almost became a German-speaking country

German school children, when starting to learn English, are told that German almost became the official language of the U.S. in 1794, losing out by just one vote. According to the U.S. Library of Congress, this is nothing but a silly myth that refuses to die.

The Library of Congress first began to receive inquiries about it during the late 1930s, when Nazi propagandists were hard at work trying to convince the world that America had almost been a German-speaking country. The story gained such momentum over the years that the Congressional Research Service looked into it in 1982. Here's what really happened.

In 1794, some German settlers in Virginia petitioned the U.S. Congress to have certain federal statutes translated into German and printed in both languages. The petition was referred to a committee, which — by a margin of one vote — rejected it.

There are distinct differences between German and American communication styles, which often cause significant misunderstandings. As this chapter explains, German business conversation places strong emphasis on content and downplays personal relationships in order to appear *credible* and *objective*. Americans, on the other hand, accentuate both the content and the personal in order to *be liked and socially accepted.* *

Communication in Germany

Back in the 1880s, Mark Twain wrote a humorous essay entitled "The Awful German Language". In it, he complained that the average sentence in a German newspaper was a monstrosity with 14 or 15 subjects and an equal number of subordinate clauses. But the worst sin the Germans committed was to put the main verb at the very end of the sentence. Twain concluded that learning the language was almost impossible for a foreigner.

Although Twain's critique on the German language was obviously a gross

---

*) See Appendix C, pg. 104 for a more detailed explanation

exaggeration, there's some truth in what he wrote. Language is a direct reflection of culture and here we can see the German "need" to over-analyse things. The communication style tends to be explicit, fact-oriented and somewhat academic. Germans are taught that the more complicated something is, the more valuable the idea must be. Being very much to the point is regarded as simple-minded by Germans, not worthy of serious consideration.

This is changing however. Not too long ago, the author met a German researcher who needed to translate a paper into English for a speech at an international conference. It was written in a stuffy, abstract style. The author asked him to say in *simple* English, what each sentence meant. The researcher protested, claiming his English wasn't sufficient, but agreed to try. Thus, the paper was translated into what he called "too simple English".

Two weeks later he gave his speech and, to his astonishment, participants came up and congratulated him on his clear, direct style. Later, when he had to give the same speech in German, he took the *English version* and translated it word for word into German! He had become a convert to clarity and conciseness. (It should be noted that large German companies now require that English be used in more and more meetings and correspondence, making for a lighter style of expression. The German language is also becoming saturated with English words, leading pundits to call it *Denglish*, a contraction of *Deutsch* and *English*.)

Detailed explanations

The German style is to fill each part of an explanation with details to avoid uncertainty and ambiguity. Being fearful that not enough is expressed, Germans tend to provide more information than required. A major article in *Der Spiegel* is generally two to three times longer than one found in *Newsweek* or *Time*. This need for detailed background information eliminates uncertainty by focusing on many bits of information.

The approach extends to presentations. The German manner is direct, analytical. The term *zum Beispiel* (for example) is used freely. Many speeches begin with the historical background of an issue, which is another example of their thoroughness. Charts and graphs are used extensively and Germans love to present one fact after another. The lengthy explanations can make non-Germans impatient and feel as if they're being treated with condescension.

Confrontational and direct

The main objective in a German conversation is to get at the truth of an issue. Germans value frankness and are not afraid to explore all sides of a topic, even if it means being unpleasant and hurting other people's feelings. They are generally more direct than Americans, especially when it comes to stating facts, offering criticism and giving commands. Americans often find this style overly-aggressive and even impolite.

Another aspect of directness is the frequent use of the modal verbs *müssen* and *sollen*. Germans find it perfectly normal to say "*Das muß so sein*", ("It must be so."). Americans would more likely use the diplomatic phrase "*It would be better if we could do it this way*", downgrading the intensity. Likewise, when ordering in a restaurant, Germans use the imperative "*Bringen Sie mir zwei Bier, bitte*". ("Bring me two beers, please.") whereas Americans would use the question "*Could we have two beers, please?*".

Additionally, German words have a hard, guttural sound with sharp, yet monotone speech patterns. It's a language that sounds like it gets things done. For a non-German, though, it may come across as rough and even "domineering".

Listening habits

A recent American study found that national listening habits made a real difference in whether a product presentation were a success or a flop. The researchers noted that Germans tended to be excellent listeners, with an attention span of at least an hour, and also wanted technical documentation on a product before getting out their checkbooks. Germans weren't impressed with a 15-minute presentation and were turned off by hype and exaggeration. And they sometimes reacted angrily when humour was injected.

With Americans, the 15-minute presentation was just enough to convince them on the merits of a product. Although they wanted to have technical data, they needed to be entertained at the same time, otherwise they became bored. Essentially, the Americans required anecdotes, humour and overstatement to sell them on a merchandise.

These clashes of differences became apparent when Daimler and Chrysler first held their board meetings together. Both realized that what they thought was the "right" way of presenting a product was actually totally wrong for the other culture.

Contents more important than style

Germans communicate in a straight, non-subtle manner, where formality and social distance are emphasized. Everything must be clear and orderly. (The German commitment to *Ordnung* extends to speech; unlike English and French, Germans words are pronounced exactly as they are written.)

Their manner induces Germans to take things at face value. If an employee is to be criticized, a German manager doesn't begin by complimenting the person on his good points before bringing up negative issues. Saying something positive only to follow up with criticism leaves Germans puzzled. The positive side of being direct and frank is that it makes Germans honest in their dealings. They will never tell you something because they think it's what you wish to hear.

Facial and body language

The facial language of Germans reveals discretion and prudence toward strangers. Germans project seriousness, stiff politeness and a seeming lack of interest in their surroundings. Smiling is not common. This is not to say they're unsociable. A German smile, for example, signifies real affection, reserved mostly for family and friends.

Their body language is low-keyed, without much body movement or fanfare. In fact, it reveals little. In business, respect and reward are given to those who exhibit confidence, control and mastery of their speciality. A firm, no-nonsense handshake is a sign of strength. Too much gesticulating or laughing is considered inappropriate.

American Communication Style

American speech, like German, is low-context, what is said is what is meant. "No" means "no", with no room for interpretation. Americans get straight to the point and want to know the intentions of others. Yet, at the same time, they want to be liked. This explains why they are more direct than Germans when it comes to expressing pleasure, giving compliments or revealing personal details to people they don't know well.

Simplicity

Whereas German thinking emphasizes complicated sentences, American students are taught that good writing is simplicity. Americans are time-conscious ("time is money") and their speech and writing patterns are generally concise. Communication is based on pragmatic thinking, like newspaper headlines — short and to the point. A line of thought is conceived in terms of efficiency: the shortest distance between two points is a straight line.

Not much time is spent on developing complicated, philosophical ideas, as it is thought to be inefficient. Americans usually only want the essential information.

The computer acronym WYSIWYG (what you see is what you get) reflects this straightforward attitude.

Although many say this leads to superficiality, a pragmatic communication style has its positive side. Americans are very good at rapid-fire, improvisational speaking. In meetings, they are able to toss wild and often nonsensical ideas around. Commonly known as brainstorming, it comes as second-nature to most Americans, part of "thinking on one's feet". Germans sometimes still have difficulty with the instantaneous spitting out of ideas.

Most Americans are not subtle in their conversations. Thoughts aren't generally carried to the second, let alone the third degree. It is for this reason they may feel uncomfortable with refined, indirect statements and often miss nonverbal cues, such as a slight shift in tone or a subtle change in body posture or breathing. When an European is trying to discretely get the message across that something is wrong, an American may not catch on. And missed hints can cause explosive situations.

Exaggeration and humor

Americans love to overstate things, all related to their infinite optimism and constant need to sell themselves. Their enthusiasm, for example, can reach levels of absurdity. (It's *fantastic* to see you again. *Wow*, you look *great!*) This can be seen in advertising hype. The Apple Company not only said that their MacIntosh computers were the fastest, but also made fun of the competition's Pentium-run computers by portraying them as snails. Germans are uncomfortable with this sort of showmanship; it is not highly regarded and, until very recently, was illegal in Germany.

Being optimistic by nature, Americans like to use humour in their conversations. To have a good sense of humour is a must if someone wants to get ahead. An effective speech usually begins with an anecdote or joke. At a social gathering or party, Americans tend to chit-chat, a light form of small talk and usually avoid any form of serious or intellectual discussions.

Facial and body language

The facial language of an American is one of animation, projecting openness, friendliness, optimism and vitality. Their body language is easy to read, an extension of being direct. It's a culture that doesn't support deception. If an American feels tired at the end of an evening party, he may yawn openly and look at you with half-closed eyes and boredom. If he's in a hurry, he'll look at his watch to signal that a meeting has gone on too long. Americans are more likely to "tell it like it is". Discretion is not one of their best qualities.

Summary of Language and Communication

Germans tend to be	Americans tend to be
— complicated	— simple
— detailed	— concise
— overly-analytical	— telegraphic
— formal	— informal
— excellent listeners	— easily bored
— serious	— humorous
— factual	— exaggerative
— reserved	— friendly
— direct, want to be credibile	— at times non-confrontational, want to be liked

Discussion Questions

1.   Discuss the possible problems Germans and Americans can have in communicating with each other.

2.   What advice on speaking English could you give an American who must negotiate with a German?

3.   Do you believe, that with more contact with Americans, Germans might start using humor and jokes in their speeches?

6.   "The Internet and e-mail are making it easier to communicate with people across cultures". Do you agree or disagree? Why?

Chapter 6

Lawsuits and Ethics

German automobile manufacturer penalized $2,004,000 for repainting a new car

In 1990, Dr. Ira Gore bought a luxury German car from his dealer in Birmingham, Alabama. Nine months later, a body shop told him his car's paint job had been partially refinished after shipment from Germany. Cars often suffer minor damage in transit and American car dealers touch them up so there are virtually no visible marks.

Dr. Gore's lawyer suggested he sue the manufacturer for failing to disclose the touch-up job. Dr. Gore went to court and a jury awarded him $4,000 in compensatory damages and $4 million in punitive damages. Later, the Alabama Supreme Court decided this was excessive and reduced the payout to "only" $2 million.

The jury reached its verdict based on evidence that the German car manufacturer had touched-up 1,000 cars in the previous ten years. The Alabama jurors were punishing the car company for failing to disclose the practice.

from The Wall Street Journal, *1995*

America's Love of Lawsuits

Nothing is more striking to a visitor to the U.S. than the over-abundance of lawyers and lawsuits. Many critics believe the reason there's so much "hair-trigger suing" is because there are so many lawyers. The country has four times more of them per capita than Germany. Also, they're willing to work for free in exchange for a percentage of whatever money is eventually won (a practice forbidden in Germany). This leads to a lot of absurd litigations.

One of the most famous examples is the $3 million awarded to a woman who spilt hot coffee on her hand at a McDonald's restaurant. Such mega-settlements encourage those with minor — or non-existent injuries — to contact a lawyer in hope of winning a similar "jackpot".

Why does the American justice system permit such preposterous lawsuits? Is it simply because there are too many hungry lawyers who need to create work for themselves? Those who have studied the problem say the answer is to be found in the Seventh Amendment of the U.S. Constitution. It states that any citizen has the right to present his or her case in front of twelve peers, twelve average citizens — the jury.

The American Jury System

Before discussing the jury system in America, some history is necessary. The U.S. judicial concept is based on Anglo-Saxon common law. All legal decisions are rendered by judges, not legislators, and are bound by precedent (previous cases). This is in contrast with Western Europe, which the legal system is borrowed from Roman law. Laws are written by professional jurists, a sort of state-controlled bureaucracy, as opposed to judge-made "interpretations".

Anglo-Saxon common law derives its structure from the *Magna Carta*, signed by King John of England in 1215. Of the 61 clauses, the most important one was "No freeman shall be captured or imprisoned (...) except by lawful judgement of his peers or by the law of the land." The "jury" was born.

By the 18th century, it had become an important protection against judicial and administrative tyranny. The institution spread to the territories colonized by England.

After the creation of the U.S. Constitution in 1787, Americans added a Bill of Rights to ensure free speech, freedom of the press and of religion, protection against "cruel and unusual punishment" and against unreasonable search or seizure. The Seventh Amendment guarantees citizens the right to trial by peers for most civil and criminal cases.

Jury trial was also widely adopted on the European continent in the 19th century, but only for criminal cases. After World War I, the custom was largely abandoned in Europe (Germany in 1924) in favor of a mixed jury, on which judges sit together with average people. Even in England, where it originated, the "layman jury" is now used only in a small percentage of cases.

Due to the Seventh Amendment in the Bill of Rights, the United States is the only country in the world that has maintained the jury system for both criminal and civil cases. It is estimated that some 220,000 jury trials are conducted each year (over 90% of all jury trials in the world).

As there has been a litigation explosion in the past 20 years, there is now a movement to abolish trial by jury in civil cases. The main argument is that a jury relies on amateurs who are emotionally swayed by unscrupulous lawyers and thus incapable of making reasonable cash assessments of damages. It would be better, so the argument goes, to permit a disciplined and experienced judge to decide if there is fault and, once fault is established, what constitutes a fair settlement. German courts use this method.

Most American lawyers, who have a vested interest in the system, are vehemently opposed to change. They argue that some decisions have forced businesses worldwide to change the ways in which they operate. Without the jury system, Ralph Nader might not have been successful in his suit against G.M.'s ill-conceived Corvair in the 1960s and car companies worldwide would have been less inclined to worry about safety issues.

Similarly, civil lawsuits are now forcing tobacco companies to pay billions of dollars in fines with much of the money going toward medical treatment for smokers. These suits are now having international repercussions.

Arguing further, American lawyers say that the justice rendered by juries has made the "little guy" a force to reckon with. As people feel more alienated from their elected representatives and government bureaucracies — and increasingly powerless in the hands of large corporations — the one place where they can still make themselves heard is the jury system. Taking away that right would be destroying a part of the American democratic ideal for most citizens.

Legal observers from Canada and Europe don't at all agree. They point out that jury settlements have become so huge that many American companies are reluctant to put out new products for fear of suits. Likewise, certain professionals, such as gynecologists and obstetricians, normally pay over $250,000 in yearly insurance premiums just to protect themselves against lawsuits. In the end, it raises the price for everything, hurting everyone.

The Gap between Americans and Europeans concerning Business Ethics

The norms of ethical behavior in business vary widely on either side of the Atlantic. While interest in business ethics and regulatory rules and standards have increased considerably in Europe in the last ten years, the latter in no way approaches the United States in persistent public concern with the morality of business behavior. The most recent example is the adoption of the Sarbanes-Oxley Act in 2003, following the Enron and WorldCom finance scandals, which required CEOs and CFOs to swear that their financial reports are accurate.

The bribery scandal (whereby the International Olympic Committee awarded Salt Lake City the 2002 Winter Games) is another example. The F.B.I and the state police were called in to investigate. Although Europeans would agree there was wrongdoing, most were surprised to learn that Utah Olympic Committee officials risked spending time in prison.

The problem of sexual harassment also shows the contrast between American standards of conduct and those of European nations. To demonstrate that the problem won't be taken lightly, the U.S. Supreme Court ruled that the company, not the individual, is legally and financially responsible for unacceptable behavior toward colleagues of the opposite sex. Mitsubishi had to pay $33 million in compensation to 300 women for having allowed sexual misconduct by male employees at its Illinois plant.

The American obsession with exposing unethical practices and punishing people with prison terms or heavy financial penalties puzzles foreigners. When asked why they are such extremists, Americans simply answer that they expect proper behavior on the part of companies. These moralistic attitudes have their roots in America's cultural past.

The United States was founded, in large part, by dissenting sects who broke off from mainstream Protestant movements (such as the Church of England) because they felt the latters' morals weren't severe enough. Not only was one expected to obtain God's salvation by creating wealth, but one had to do so in an absolutely ethical manner, "no lying or cheating". Even today, Americans are likely to believe that business and honesty go hand in hand. The $8 billion lawsuit by investor Kirk Kerkorian against Daimler/Chrysler for false statements at the time of the merger can be largely understood in this context.

Contrast this with the moral standards of European business. Instead of believing that man could be changed for the better, as the dissenting sects did in America, the Old World takes a more fatalistic view of man. "Can the leopard change his spots?" sums up the idea that man can't change his nature and there will always be bad along with good.

Additionally, Europeans have a legacy of aristocratic, pre-capitalist values, which tend to view the pursuit of profit (and even of being in business) as beneath one's dignity. To make money is, in itself, a somewhat dubious undertaking. When a manager or company is caught paying money under the table to gain a contract, Europeans are less likely to be outraged. In fact, until 1998, income tax authorities accepted most bribes as a deductible business expense in both France and Germany.

Americans take great pride in their individualism and often look with suspicion on authority. Basically, Americans see themselves first as individuals and secondarily as members of a family, group or organization. Not surprisingly, a company's objectives and those of an individual may come into conflict. American values encourage individuals to report unethical activities. There are regulatory statutes on whistle-blowers, which protect individuals who publicly expose the illegal activities of an organization or corporation.

In contrast, Europeans are more likely to make decisions according to community or company norms, not personal beliefs. Workers usually feel a greater sense of loyalty toward the firm. Whistle-blowers are seen as outsiders rather than heroes.

Another major difference between the American and European approaches is the role of law and formal rules. Americans tend to believe that business ethics can be reduced to principles and guidelines, a sort of "morality checklist". This inclination to think in terms of rules has given rise to corporate codes of conduct, which, critics point out, contribute to a "deresponsibilization" of the individual. Like a machine, a person need only apply the rules he or she has learned, responding in a "corporate" way.

Europeans, for the most part, are appalled at such automatic devices and continually surprised that American executives sincerely believe that adopting an "ethical code" will actually change employee behavior. They tend to view this as excessively naive and prefer to be guided by informal mechanisms of social control within the company.

Americans also seem to feel that their own rules and ethics should be applied throughout the world, something which irritates Europeans. An example of this is the Foreign Corrupt Practices Act (FCPA) of 1977, which makes it a crime for a U.S. company to offer payments to influence the actions of foreign executives or politicians. The penalties include fines and possible prison terms. (It should be noted that in February 1999, under strong pressure from the U. S., the European Union signed an agreement outlawing bribes.)

These major divergences in outlook demonstrate that the ethical gap between American and European business practices remains large. Executives from both continents have largely ignored the subject until now. A better appreciation of the differences in the legal and cultural context of business is needed to help international managers work together more effectively.

Summary of Lawsuits

German legal system

— governed by Roman law

— laws made by professional jurists

— jury trial for criminal cases only

— layman jury abolished in 1924 (in favor of
   a mixed jury)

— monetary settlements made only by experienced judge

— makes it more difficult to start a new business

— is generally not a factor in doing business

American legal system

— governed by common law

— laws are judge-made "interpretations"

— jury trial for both civil and criminal cases

— guaranteed right to layman jury (7th
   amendment in 1787)

— monetary settlements made by common people

— makes it easier to start a new business

— can involve major costs for doing business

Summary of Business Ethics

Germans tend to be

— less concerned about business behavior

— more fatalistic about the nature of man

— less moralistic toward companies

— guided by community norms and traditions

— less likely to report unethical behavior

— guided by informal codes

Americans tend to be

— more insistent on proper business behavior

— influenced by moralistic thinking

— pro-business (with honesty)

— guided by the individual's conscience

— more likely to report unethical behavior

— often influenced by "morality checklists"

Discussion Questions

1. What role does the jury system play in American culture?

2. What do you think would happen if Germany adopted the American "layman jury" ?

3. Where do the moralistic attitudes of the Americans originate?

4. Why do ethics create conflict?

5. How are ethics intimately connected to culture?

Chapter 7

The Interculturally-Competent Person

Understanding Others

"To understand a particular group of people, one should try to enter, as much as possible, into the historical and cultural context of these people and the country they live in...Now, this is not easy. There is something confusing in all this: a particular incident, which seems obvious to us, is not perceived by the others as the same...To rid oneself of the frustration one feels, it is just enough to think...that the other one has not received the same conditioning as we have and he can not escape his own conditioning. Whatever the future holds for us, each group of people, each country is different from the others...by its ways of observing things, of living and thinking. In order to understand the others, we should use their language, whenever it is possible. I wish to say: not only the totality of the words that form their language, but also the language of their spirit and their heart. It is an absolute necessity. This doesn't consist of only appealing to logic and reason. It consists of an emotional opening to the others."

Jawaharlal Nehru, Visit to America

Over 125 years ago, Jules Verne wrote *Around the World in 80 Days*. At the time of its appearance, the book generated great excitement: travelling around the world in that short a time was considered revolutionary. Today we can travel from New York to Frankfurt in seven hours. We can also communicate instantaneously, via telephone or e-mail, from anywhere to anywhere else. Enhancements in communications and transportation allow us immediate contact worldwide, laying the groundwork for globalization.

While these changes may have enriched our lives, they have created complexity. Almost without realizing it, we have shifted into a new mode of living where cross-cultural contact has become a daily occurrence. This is a new phenomenon. Looking back over most of human history, we find that cross-cultural contact has more often than not been characterized by bloodshed, oppression, even genocide. Groups sought similarity, people like themselves. If contact was made with "strangers", it was usually for reasons of trade or war.

Now we're suddenly expected to live in harmony with other groups. To say that most of us haven't been prepared is an understatement. Our old habit of protecting our tribe, of living in splendid isolation, has become dysfunctional in the era of globalization. What is called for as we reach the third millennium is cross-cultural sensitivity.

How does this sensitivity come about? Researcher Milton Bennett sees the development of intercultural competence as a sequence of six subjective states.

Ethnocentric stages

1. *Denial: can't perceive any differences — the unconscious assumption that one's own reality is everybody's reality .*
   Example: An American tourist in Munich after three days: "It's like New York — lots of buildings, too many cars, McDonald's."
2. *Defensive: difference is perceived as threatening*
   Example: A German manager in Detroit after one month: "Americans are superficial and uncultivated."
3. *Minimization: differences are trivialized*
   Example: An American banker in Frankfurt after three months: "We bankers are the same all over the world."

Ethnorelative stages

4. *Acceptance: appreciation of cultural differences*
   Example: A German salesman arriving in Los Angeles: "Where can I learn more about American culture to be more effective in my communication?"
5. *Adaptation: adjusting to cultural differences*
   Example: An American student at the University of Tübingen after one year:
   "The more I understand this culture, the better I get at the language."
6. *Integration: incorporating cultural differences*
   Example: A German executive who has lived in New York for ten years: "I truly enjoy participating fully in both of my cultures."

Once the sixth stage has been attained, one can be described as an interculturally-competent person. But what are the characteristics?

To begin with, the person no longer feels solely attached to his or her original cultural group. He or she has gone beyond the group's value-system and is able to recognize and adapt to other cultural contexts.

The interculturally-competent person doesn't think in ethnocentric terms but is a "cross-cultural swinger", juggling two or more competing value-systems. Such a person is capable of seeing and feeling the relativity of beliefs — there is no absolute standard of "rightness". It's an intellectual and emotional opening to others through which one embraces the change necessary for growth and generally feels free to be different.

In the vast majority of cases, the person speaks more than one language, is not limited to a single linguistic reality. By being open-minded and receptive toward other cultures, a person automatically learns much more about him- or herself.

Ultimately, this is a person who can understand and reconcile the dilemmas of the human condition in different contexts. For example, when an American is confronted with the German need for perfection, it is understood as a real — not a frivolous — concern.

This is not to say that the person has lost his or her values. One always preserves a certain "ethnocentrism", maintaining certain fundamental attitudes while possessing an "other-culture awareness" (a recognition and acceptance of different values). It's perfectly natural to remain attached to one's own cultural group; a person needs a healthy ego based on fundamental attitudes toward life.

For any company to survive, let alone flourish in the future, its perspectives must be global. We are being forced to move from the "nationalistic" mode toward a greater recognition and acceptance of other ways of living. As we can never know a different culture fully, the goal is to raise our sensitivity and reach some degree of cross-cultural comprehension.

If one accepts the premise that globalization is the future, then it is clear corporations must re-engineer their organizational processes and re-equip their personnel with intercultural communication skills. Only through an acceleration of global learning-curves and a broadening of information streambeds will companies obtain a competitive edge in today's increasingly complex world.

Characteristics of an interculturally-competent person

     — No longer solely attached to original cultural group

     — Feels the relativity of values

     — Is a "cross-cultural swinger"

     — Is usually able to communicate in more than one language

     — Can understand human dilemmas in different cultural contexts

     — Keeps a certain "ethnocentrism" as well as "other-culture awareness"

Discussion Questions

1. Re-read Jawaharta Nehru's *Understanding Others.* What is his main message? Why does it have universal appeal?

2. Do you agree that living solely in one's cultural group has become dysfunctional in this era of globalization?

3. What are the personal attributes of an interculturally-competent person? Is this the ideal model for the successful merging of American and German companies?

4. In your opinion, what are the major changes that will affect cross-cultural management and organizational behavior in the next ten years? In the next 20 years?

Appendix

Epilogue to the 2003 Edition

Much has transpired in the business worlds of the United States and Germany in the last five years. Globalization, the continuing evolution of information technology, international terrorism and, more recently, the 21st-century version of "insider trading", all have shaped a variety of changes which are on-going and increasingly profound.

Surprisingly, the American corporate community has been most affected not by the September 11 terrorist attacks but the spectacular series of scandals exemplified by the bankruptcies of Enron and WorldCom. Flagrantly dishonest bookkeeping and stock-market disinformation have forced Washington to adopt a law requiring CEOs and CFOs to swear that their financial reports are accurate. Those caught cheating will now face up to $5 million in fines and 20 years in prison.

However this doesn't imply any real questioning of the U.S. business philosophy "maximum profit whatever the cost". Rather, it's a simple tightening of the rules designed, more than anything, to boost public confidence and keep the system chugging along as before.

Less remarked — but more startling — is the slow reshaping of German business culture along American lines. This involves no less an issue than that of national identity as a whole. Or, as some ask, "What is a German today?"

Soul-searching is obviously something Germany has done a lot of since the end of World War II. World War II. The traditional values — order, duty and discipline — have been examined and debated for nearly three generations. Despite this, they are still cherished in the heart and form the watchwords of German business. The American boom-and-bust mentality has, for the most part, remained foreign. As a Deutsche Bank VP said a decade ago, "We expect a return of perhaps 10% but know it is to be year after year…In the U.S., they double profits one year and go bankrupt the next!"

This seems now to be changing. The *world's* business is more and more geared toward speed and flexibility, short-term results under shareholder swords-of-Damocles. Like it or not, Germans have no choice but to follow the hard-line business lead. It's a heart-rending exercise indeed. The country underwent a sea of change in 1945 and another in 1989. This third "culture shock", that of transnational capitalism, will be the most difficult. Especially since the leitmotiv involved--*maximum profit*--goes against both traditional values and their cherished social market economy (*soziale Marktwirtschaft*).

To understand how these values are being put to question, a short historical review is necessary. The modern German mindset is made up of a centuries-old authoritarian system mixed with the democratic values and promise of "freedom" introduced by the Americans after the war. Some call it *Verinnerlichung*, the internalization of American influences, a process which began immediately after Germany surrendered to the Allied forces in 1945.

As opposed to the British, the French and the Russians, Americans were more forgiving. As inhabitants of a separate continent they were better able to overlook the destruction caused by the Nazi regime. And they were the only country able to provide Germany with the money necessary to rebuild. The Marshall Plan was not without strings, of course, the most important being the creation of truly democratic institutions.

Although the German elite found American cultural values to be vulgar and "disorderly", the former had absolutely no moral authority to offer an alternative. WW II, and especially the Holocaust, had stripped them of respect. No wonder, therefore, that the post-war generation agreed with Joschka Fischer, the extremely popular Foreign Minister, when he called the U.S. an ersatz father offering a system where all citizens were equal and individual freedom was possible.

American "casualness" (in dress, in speech) and anti-authoritarian attitudes became the nightmare of Germany's elite. As Joschka Fischer put it, "Germans today are the children of the Nazis as well as the Americans. Hitler's terrible crimes will have an impact on Germans for generations. But the Americans taught the Germans democratic culture, upon which a heritage can be built."

It is precisely this mixture of German and American values that has made the culture more open and, therefore, more vulnerable in the modern world. Germany was forced to abandon many of its traditional beliefs virtually overnight. But the philosophical substitution — *soziale Marktwirtschaft*, only just achieved with the fall of the Berlin Wall, is suddenly no longer enough. It is time to change again, to learn a new set of values.

For example, instilled deeply in the German mind is the idea that one must always respect and obey rules. It is a desire for order--*Ordnung muss sein*--and, in fact, a formula for social harmony. Now Germans are torn between their need for "*Ordnung*" and pragmatic solutions to the disorderly, accelerating spiral of the planet's affairs in the year 2003. A trivial but telling example is the city of Düsseldorf, where urbanization and economic success have engendered a deluge of cars competing daily for very few parking spaces. Frustrated Germans, who have seen the situation get worse and worse over the years, have finally begun parking on the sidewalks. This is to say that Germans are now parking like Parisians, surely not a good sign! (And the Germans--who have kept things bottled up for so long--actually *outdo* the French; they often double-park, even when it means blocking the street tram.)

The *consensus principle* is another example, having a long tradition in Germany but it, too, has been considerably weakened over the last five years. First introduced in 1871 by Otto von Bismarck, it's based on a "social partnership ", an association of labor, business and government. Underlying this was the tenet that management would share profits with its workers and not grant itself excessive rewards.

But globalization, as well as the high visibility of American management practices, led many German CEOs to go on a grab-it-all spree. In July 2002, *Manager Magazin* showed how the salaries of corporate bosses have exploded without any sort of parallel increase in company value. The most flagrant example is that of *Deutsche Telekom*'s former CEO Ron Sommer and his Board of Directors, who voted themselves a 90% raise even as the company's stock value was in the process of losing 350 billion Euros! It's fairly obvious that the "consensus principle" has been rendered all but obsolete.

According to the latest polls, young Germans, like their American counterparts, are more conformist than their parents. Paradoxically, the same *20-something* generation celebrates individualism and is more optimistic. Also, most speak English fairly well. Like their American counterparts, they want to have fun, go to Burger King, watch MTV...

Germany's young people demonstrate that the line between American and German culture not only overlaps but is disappearing. This is no more apparent than on television (where else?), which increasingly mirrors U.S. fare. Two very popular talk-show hosts, Harald Schmidt and Stefan Raab, conduct "loony" interviews, guests perform "nutty" acts, and everyone agrees to do something very un-German indeed: they make fun of themselves. As *Der Spiegel* noted, "The Copernican turning-point for German humor has already begun."

Still, the biggest social earthquake may well be that Germans are now forced to admit their school system is no longer the best. Forty years ago, international experts all agreed, Germany was at the top in both primary and secondary education. Since then, however, countries such as Finland, Canada and Korea have surged ahead, something clearly demonstrated in the 2001 PISA results. Germany's students, as a whole, performed slightly *below* the international average.

Once the shock subsided, German educators learned that their country was spending less per capita than the average OECD nation, especially at the elementary level. At the same time, the massive influx of immigrant children (who, in many cases, hadn't mastered the language) brought down the national score. Teachers are unanimous in saying that Germany has to change its priorities and invest more in kindergartens and primary schools to make sure *all* children can read and write properly.

The fundamental purpose of this book is to examine our inner values and their impact on cross-cultural communications. That these attitudes are fluid, that *the world* is contracting, that both the U.S. and Germany are constantly re-inventing themselves, makes any affirmation subject to revision. Yet, it is only by examining context that the reader will be able to grasp the deeper and often contradictory manner in which American and German business cultures *really* operate.

B. Cross-Cultural Case Studies

1.

Country: USA

Issue: Sexual Harassment

Jürgen is a young German executive, working at his company's subsidiary plant in Chicago. Many of his American co-workers are women. Although he is not quite used to seeing so many females in executive positions, he accepts the fact and actually finds it pleasant.

He is aware that overt flirting is a touchy subject in American business circles (the U.S. Supreme Court has ruled that the company, not the individual, is legally and financially responsible for unacceptable behavior toward colleagues of the opposite sex). But Jürgen is young and single and finds Monica quite attractive. Although flirting is harmless in itself, this could lead to complications. Jürgen is not sure how he should handle the situation.

What would you consider to be the best approach?
1. Try to assess your chances with Monica through physical contact.
2. Tactfully compliment Monica on her smile, her hair or her clothes.
3. Compliment her that she is good at her job.

Answers:
1. This is obviously wrong.
2. This is acceptable, provided it is done in good taste.
3. This is the safest and a way to cultivate a relationship.

Some helpful information:

Sexual harassment is defined by law as "unwelcome sexual advances, requests for sexual favors and other verbal or physical conduct of a sexual nature." The following could constitute sexual harassment, according to the *Harvard Business Review:*
1. My supervisor eyes me up and down, making me feel uncomfortable.
2. My supervisor puts his hand on my arm when making a point.
3. My supervisor makes sexual remarks or jokes.
4. I get patted or pinched by my supervisor.
5. My boss told me it would be good for my career if I went out with him.

These acts impose absolute liability on a company for the acts of supervisors, regardless of whether the conduct was known to — or, in fact, forbidden by — that company. Co-workers are also liable, even if the employer takes immediate action. However, their penalties are less severe (usually constituting fines).

2.

Country: USA

Issue: Different concepts of friendship

Manfred Schneider, on a flight to Detroit, meets Bob Clyde, an American executive from the same company. Bob introduces Manfred to his wife at the airport saying: "Honey, I'd like you to meet my friend Manfred. We have just met on the plane". Manfred is surprised to be called a friend; he hasn't even had time to consider the possibility. Before they go their separate ways, they exchange phone numbers, promising to call each other.

Two weeks later, Bob sees Manfred at the company cafeteria. Although the latter smiles and says "hi" in a friendly manner, he passes Bob's table to sit with other people. Bob is perplexed and feels somewhat hurt. He wonders what has happened.

It is possible that:
1. Manfred received an unimpressive picture of him and decided to discontinue the "friendship".
2. Although Manfred seemed to enjoy conversing with Bob on the plane, it wasn't that meaningful to him. Manfred didn't think he was obliged to accept friendship at such short notice.
3. Manfred is not influenced by first impressions.

Answers:

The most likely is number two. Because of his cultural upbringing, Manfred would have to get to know Bob better before considering friendship.

3.

Country: USA

Issue: Punctuality

Joachim Teufel has been working for some months in his company's newly-acquired research and development lab in Santa Barbara, California. He was sent there to oversee operations. His American counterpart, Jim Higgins, has been working closely with him on several projects.

Although Joachim likes Jim's friendliness, vitality and perceptiveness, the latter has one habit that bothers Joachim's sense of order. Just before they attend a meeting, Jim always seems to need to make an important telephone call or finish writing a letter. As a result, he's usually late. Joachim can't understand Jim's poor time-management.

What's the explanation?

1. People in southern California are "laid back" and don't care about punctuality.
2. Americans like to do many things at once and often end up being late because of their conflicting schedules.
3. It makes a good impression to be late (in order to portray oneself as being very busy).

Answers:

1. This is unlikely. As in Germany, punctuality has the same value in the U.S., including southern California.
2. This is the principle reason for his tardiness. Americans, by nature, try to do as much as possible within a certain time. The Germans also want to accomplish a lot but they systematically plan every activity so as to avoid conflicting schedules as much as possible. Americans don't plan as carefully, leading to situations where they they have much to do at the same time.
3. This is absolutely false. Although Americans put a high value on appearance and image, it's highly unlikely that they would manipulate a situation in this fashion.

4.

Country: Germany

Issue: German thoroughness

Michael Hill and George Brown are American engineers working in their company's subsidiary in Frankfurt. They were recently assigned to help two German engineers to choose a new software program that would help coordinate their company's services.

Both Michael and George found their German colleagues were asking too many "basic" questions and wasting everybody's time by spinning out hypothetical situations. Wanting to demonstrate American pragmatism and straightforwardness, they reached a deal with a software company only after two days. The Germans were pleasantly surprised by the speed of the Americans. Although they wanted to look at alternatives, the Germans reluctantly approved the purchase.

A few days after the software was introduced, it became clear that there were severe compatibility problems. The program had to be withdrawn and the team had to meet again to find a new solution.

What happened here?

1. The Americans wanted to show that an adequate solution could be found without "excessive German thoroughness".
2. Americans don't like to systematically think through complex problems, prefering quick solutions.
3. Americans take the approach, "Let's try this out and, if it doesn't work, we'll look for another alternative".
4. The Americans didn't collected enough information to determine the correct needs of the company.

Answers:

1. This is a possibility. However, Americans can be just as thorough as Germans when a situation calls for it.
2. This is basically wrong. Some of the best scientific investigations in the world come from U.S. research centers. While Americans may be too quick in problem-solving, this doesn't at all mean that they can't think through problems.
3. This is typical of the American thought process and the most likely explanation. Americans often use trial-by-error methodology (even if it proves to be more expensive in the long run).
4. This explanation, closely related to the third answer, is also possible. Germans, by nature, spend more time analyzing and evaluating alternatives. Once they think they have a decent answer, Americans stop examining alternatives and quickly move forward.

5.

Country: USA

Issue: Teamwork

Ralf Beutel has been sent by his Hamburg-based shipping company to their American subsidiary in San Francisco. He finds the city agreeable, likes the working conditions and the way Americans seem to get along so well with one another.

He has just been given a major project by the Hamburg office to see if the German method of loading cargo will work in an American port. As he likes working with Chris and Jerry, two of his American colleagues, he suggests that they share responsibility for the test run. To his surprise, his colleagues don't show any enthusiasm for the suggestion. Instead, they propose that the work be divided up into three parts so that management will be able to see who did what.

What happened?

1. The American colleagues don't appreciate that a newcomer (and a foreigner) arrives at the company and wants to change their work habits.
2. Americans prefer to work alone because they can have more responsiblity and can complete the task quicker.
3. Americans don't like teamwork.

Answers:

1. While Germans might think this answer is correct, it generally isn't valid in the U.S. Of course, people in any cultural setting are wary of a newcomer. Unlike Germany, however, changing jobs often is not unusual and Americans are less reticent toward new co-workers. Also, when a new employee demonstrates initiative and a desire to improve working conditions, it's viewed in a positive light.
2. This is the most likely explanation. Americans prefer to work alone rather than in a group. Although there is a higher risk in having sole responsiblity, there is also more freedom in decision-making and a greater probability that one will be rewarded for individual performance.
3. This is absolutely wrong. Americans do work in teams but have a different concept of what teamwork means. For them, it's a clear division of tasks while getting along with others. What is most important

is how individual performance is perceived and judged. Germans, on the other hand, see teamwork as a mutually-supportive activity with shared responsibilities.

6.

Country: USA

Issue: Action-oriented activities

Elke Huck has been working two months at the Los Angeles subsidiary of a Swiss bank. She has made some good contacts with her American colleagues and would like to know them on a more personal level. She invites Tom, Suzanne and Kathy for dinner at her apartment.

She prepares a four-course German meal and her guests find the food delicious. After eating, Elke suggests that they all go out on the balcony and sip some German wine. As they sit around, the atmosphere turns quiet; nobody seems to have anything to say. To Elke's surprise, Tom suggests that they all go see a film at the nearby movie theater (which they agree to do).

Afterwards, Elke wonders why her guests wanted to leave so early.

What happened?

1. Her guests became bored as the evening progressed.
2. Americans are not used to sitting around and talking to people they don't know that well.
3. Her guests misunderstood the dinner invitation. Once the dinner was finished, they felt the "official" visit had come to an end and it was up to them to suggest something to do.

Answers:

1. This is highly unlikely, but is a possible explanation. Some Americans become uneasy if boredom seems to be setting in. As it's not in the nature of Americans to do nothing, a person may take the initiative and propose that the group do something together.
2. This is probably the most correct explanation. Americans like to view themselves as pro-active and efficient people, always on the go. The culture emphasizes activities that have definite goals. It goes hand in hand with their philosophical leitmotiv "the pursuit of happiness".

In the eyes of Americans, this can only be reached through concrete achievements (such as playing games, going to the movies, etc).

3. Although unlikely, this could be a possible explanation, and is related to the two previous answers. Many Americans feel that to sit around and "shoot the breeze" is not productive. So it wouldn't be unusual for someone to suggest an activity.

7.

Country: Germany

Issue: "Small-talk"

Hans Schumacher works for an American firm in hometown Düsseldorf. Many of his colleagues are expatriates with whom he gets along extremely well. Schumacher and his family were recently invited to Tom Lennon's home for a special "Mexican fiesta" evening.

Hans, Tom and their wives found the dinner very enjoyable. They talked about almost everything: the American way of life, the best places to visit in the U.S. and Germany, which country had the best beer, and so on. However, as soon as Hans tried to bring up a serious subject (such as the political direction of Germany or American social problems), his talk fell on deaf ears. Tom went back to non-controversial subjects while insisting they eat more tacos.

What happened?

1. When Americans put on a theme party, the last thing they want to talk about are society's problems. A "fiesta evening" is meant for having fun.

2. The Americans are very sensitive to issues that might in some way attack their country. Subjects such as these are avoided.

3. Americans are uninformed and badly educated when it comes to understanding and discussing issues affecting the world. To avoid being exposed as ignoramuses, they retreat to trivial themes.

4. Americans find serious subjects not worth their time.

Answers:

1. This is the most likely explanation. When Americans invite friends for a "fun" dinner, they generally don't want to be bothered with "heavy" issues. Historically, Americans have tended to avoid phiosophical discussions as

it conficts with their need to be socially accepted and pragmatic in conversation. Germans are somewhat confused by this because in their culture, rational and analytical discourse is idealized.

2. This is not the correct interpretation. Americans are not afraid to talk about their country when it concerns controversial issues. If one is invited to a "fun" party, however, it's not the right venue for this type of discussion.

3. This is absolutely wrong. While it is true that there are certain segments of American society which are really misinformed or incapable of understanding the political, economical and social forces affecting the world, this also can be said for certain segments of the population in Germany. In general, Americans sent over to represent their company are well-informed and well-educated and can actually be very interesting people to talk to.

4. Also wrong. Although Americans do tend to see problems in a more optimistic light, this should not be misinterpreted as being superficial. Americans can be very critical and thoughtful on issues when the situation calls for it.

9.

Country: USA

Issue: Autocratic rule

Reinhardt Waimer has been working for over a year in an American engineering office. Both his firm and it's U.S. partner are working on a joint-venture in China. He's found the work interesting and extremely rewarding thus far.

There is only one aspect of American business he dislikes — contradiction between apparent egalitarianism and obvious autocratic rule. On one hand, everybody is called by their first name — even the CEO — and there is no visible hierarchy. On the other hand, the directors vote themselves generous stock-options that borderline on highway robbery.

When the members of the Board are questioned about this at stockholders' meetings, they simply reply that rank has its privileges. Which include determining their own salaries.

Waimer points out these contradictions to his American colleagues but they all smile and say that it's "the American way" and, in the same breath, they wish they could do it themselves.

Why is this so?

1. Despite the appearance of equality, Americans are not so egalitarian as they pretend to be.
2. The CEO and members of the Board in U.S. culture are generally admired and seen as heros, which goes hand in hand with the saying "The business of America is business". The rules of egalitarianism don't apply.
3. What a top American executive earns has absolutely no relationship to his cooperative style.

Answers:

1. The American belief that all men are created equal has more to do with how people interact socially than with actual power and hierarchy. The big boss of a company is expected to be friendly and easy-going with everyone. At the same time, he possesses immense power and status which he can use at his discretion.
2. Although Americans have been brought up to treat everyone equally, they also have a need for role models, which represent the *American Dream*, (making it to the top of the social ladder). It is for that reason a highly successful businessperson — a Bill Gates or a Henry Ford — is admired even if he appears to be making a fabulous amount of money at the expense of others. Historically, the U.S. has been a rich land where there has been lots to go around. This explains why there is little envy in American culture (something that can be difficult for Germans to understand).
3. This answer is related to the second response.

9.

Country: Germany

Issue: Presentation style

Gerhardt Späth worked as a department leader at Baywald GmbH, one of Germany's largest chemical companies. Because he spoke English quite well, he was asked to make a presentation of his company's strategic plans and vision to a group of American chemical engineers, who were looking into the possibility of doing a joint-venture with the German company.

Gerhardt spent a lot of time preparing his speech. . He began his talk with a long overview of historical trends in the chemical industry, the consequences of globalization and why so many mergers had been taking place. Then he talked about the growth prognosis for the German and European markets and the need for the chemical industry to expand to South America and Southeast Asia. At that point, he explained why he thought the North America market would become less important in years to come, due to saturation of the market. Finally, he presented his company's financial balance-sheet, along with its strategy and future perspectives. In all, his speech was well over one hour.

While he was talking, Gerhardt noticed that his audience became fidgety after 20 minutes. Towards the end, some listeners were reading brochures or even speaking with their neighbors. He was confused and disappointed by the behavior of the American visitors.

What happened?

1. Gerhardt's prognosis that the North American market would stagnate was not appreciated.
2. The presentation was simply too long; the Americans felt that their time was being wasted.
3. The American audience expected more of an exchange of ideas, not a monologue speech.

Answers:

1. This is highly unlikely. American business executives are not afraid of hearing the truth, especially when it comes to where future investments should be made. What counts with any businessperson — whether that person be American, German, or Japanese — is an objective presentation of the facts so that rational decisions can be made.
2. This is the most likely reason. As opposed to Germans who like detailed, historical background information and are very patient while listening, Americans want a speaker to get straight to the point. Nothing is more insulting and condescending for an American than to sit through a long speech and not know where the speaker will take them until the very end of the presentation. Americans expect to be told from the start what the purpose of the presentation is and immediately hear arguments in favor of the speaker's point of view. There is no need for what Americans would call "superfluous" information. Also, Americans like humor during the talk to spice up things. In general, presentations are much shorter in the U. S. than in Germany.

3. This is also a possibility, however less so. Americans can sit through a speech provided it is short and lively. They will, however, participate gladly in a presentation, if asked to do so. They enjoy give-and-take and feel no uneasiness when arguing with a speaker. This is strongly related to the American value of egalitarianism, where everyone is viewed as a coequal.

10.

Country: USA

Issue: National pride

Wolfgang Fischer heads up research and development for one of Germany's printing presses manufacturers. He's been invited by an American producer of printing machines to have a look at their products and give his opinion of their new line.

During the tour, Wolfgang is pleasantly surprised by the innovative and creative drive of the Americans. Afterward, his hosts invite him to their office to comment on what he's seen. Noting that the Americans were quite informal in their manner, Wolfgang decides he'll act the same. Leaning back in his chair and stretching out his legs, "cowboy style", he begins his assessment in a casual manner.

He tells his audience that the American manufacturing industry has made fantastic progress, more astonishing when considering that, ten years back, their products were considered awful. He compliments them on how they've cleverly integrated computer technology into their products, something they hadn't done before, allowing them to catch up with their German competitors.

Despite all the compliments, Wolfgang has the distinct feeling that his American hosts aren't too impressed. This feeling is confirmed when they suddenly break up the meeting and offer to call him a taxi.

What happened?

1. So many compliments were made that the Americans actually felt embarrassed.
2. The compliments Wolfgang made were perceived as being condescending and insensitive.
3. Wolfgang's casualness was not at all appreciated by his American hosts.

Answers:

1. Not at all correct. Americans like being complimented and likewise love to flatter and give positive feedback to others whenever possible. Common sense tells us that if an American firm invites a foreigner to inspect their products, the least they can expect is some measure of praise for their work

2. This is probably the correct interpretation. Arriving as a foreigner and telling your host in a casual, almost disrespectful manner that their products were bad in the past, even through you're complimenting the progress made since, can be interpreted as the quintessence of insensitivity. Additionally, one should consider that Americans identify strongly with their country and understandably feel attacked and hurt when their products are described as mediocre (even if it's the truth). Extreme sensitivity is called for.

3. This could also explain the disapproval of the Americans. Even if a German is well aware of American ways, such as using slang or talking about sporting events, a German should behave as a German, especially when advice is being sought.

   To understand this more clearly, place yourself in the opposite situation. An American comes to Germany to look at your products. He speaks German well (although with an American accent). Despite this, you respect his effort for having learned the language. However, when that same person tries to imitate your slang, and be "more German than the Germans", your reaction is likely to be negative. He's trying to be somebody that he is not.

C. German and American Communication Styles

Our style of communication is in direct relationship to the values and rules of the culture in which we were raised. When interacting, most people forget that each culture has a specific set of rules. As author Greg Nees in his well-written book *Germany - Unraveling an Enigma* points out, Germans and Americans have distinct speaking styles,which often lead to subtle but significant misunderstandings (even when the two parties think they've understood each other).

German business conversation places strong emphasis on content and downplays personal relationships. As previously stated, their unconscious desire is to appear *credible* and *objective*, which tends to make their conversational style fact-oriented and somewhat pedantic. Germans are generally more direct than Americans, especially when it comes to stating facts, offering criticism and giving orders.

Americans unconsciously accentuate the personal as well as the business agenda; they want to *be liked and socially accepted*. Generally more outer-directed, they are guided less by their inner values than by the opinion of others. This makes them more direct than Germans when it comes to expressing pleasure, giving compliments or revealing personal details to people they don't know well.

If these different conversational styles are not fully understood, <u>negative stereotyping is bound to occur</u>. Americans will perceive Germans as obstinate, cold and "argumentative know-it-alls". Germans will view Americans as "naive, superficial, childish and ignorant".

Another potential problem, according to Nees, is the way Americans and Germans communicate in private and in public. It differs considerably and contributes to linguistic confusion when the two interact. To understand this, we must first look at how the individual personality is made up. Social scientist Kurt Lewin was one of the first to understand that one's personality is tightly intertwined with the social/cultural system. The following illustrations are a further development of his theories:

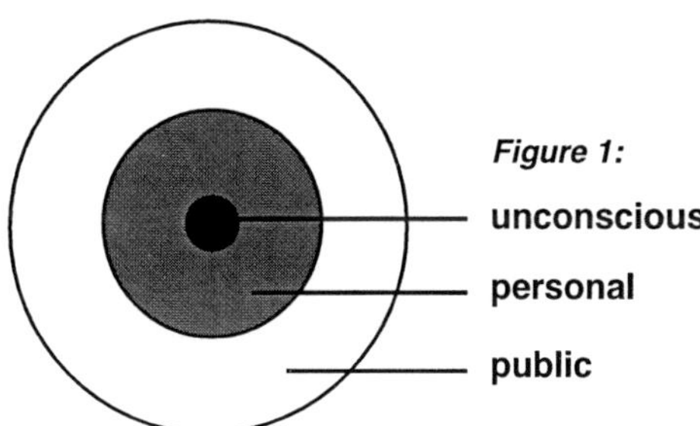

The two inner circles represent the most personal and fragile parts of an individual. These are only revealed to one's closest friends and family members. The outer circle represents the more public parts of the personality.

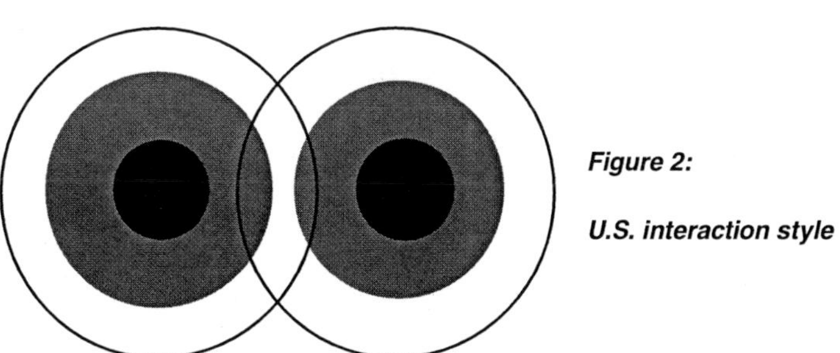

U.S. interactions are characterized by an extroverted style and a willingness to quickly move to a first-name basis. Americans display a readiness to speak openly about many things Germans would consider highly intimate (figure 2).

In Germany, there is a strong line of demarcation. This symbolizes the private/public, the *du/Sie* distinction (figure 3). In English, which has only the personal pronoun *you*, there is more overlapping. When Germans are with friends and family (figure 4), interaction tends to be more intimate than with Americans in the same situation. As Germans make such a clear differentiation between *du* and *Sie* relationships and Americans do not, misinterpretations invariably happen.

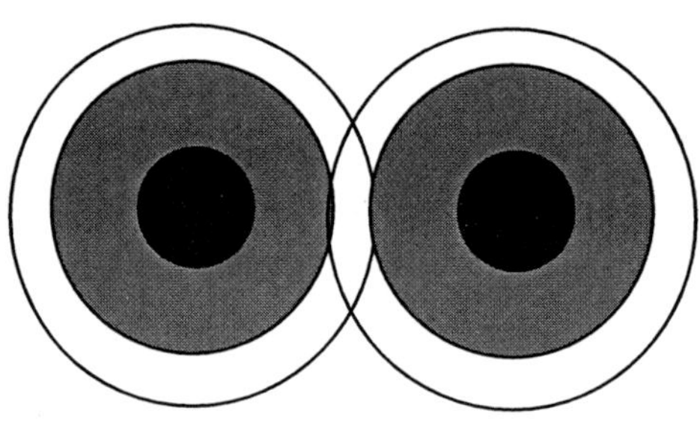

Figure 3:

German «Sie»
interaction style

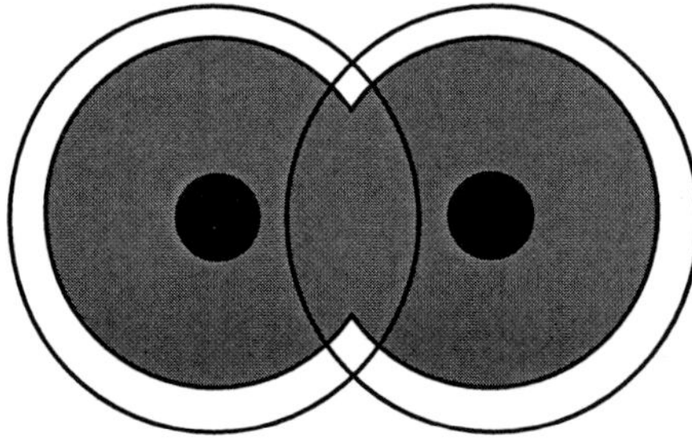

Figure 4:

German «du»
interaction style

Misunderstandings occur when a person with one conception of private/public space meets a person with a different one. This conflicting area is called the **danger zone**.

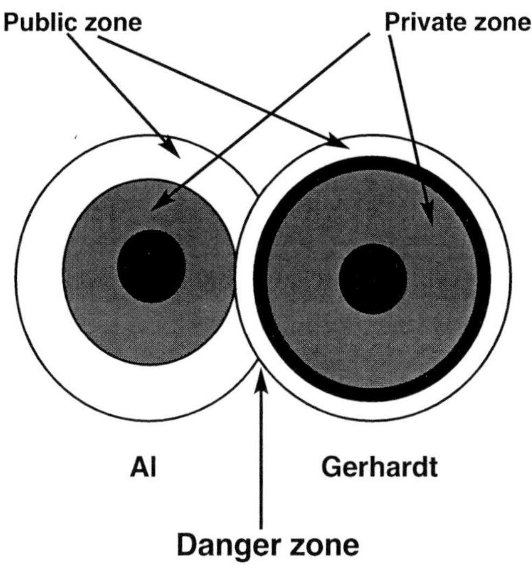

Al invites Gerhardt to his home for a barbecue and a swim in his swimming pool:

Gerhardt believes the invitation entitles him to a close-friend position. In the eyes of Al, however, Gerhardt is only entering a "public zone". If he starts to behave like an old friend, Al will be irritated.

On the other hand, since Gerhardt believes he's now within Al's "private zone," he'll feel slighted if his "friend" doesn't give him a call next time he's in town.

Gerhardt invites Al to his home for dinner:

Gerhardt offers of a lot of private information about the family, something Al may not be interested in or comfortable with. Al may also not respond in kind. At the end of the evening, Gerhardt thinks Al is superficial and Al is convinced that Gerhardt is too emotional, too "deep".

D. Problem-solving in joint German-American Teams

In 1995, German psychologist Sylvia Schroll-Machl conducted a study of why American-German projects often failed. Acting as a moderator at a German multinational corporation, she was able to observe and evaluate American and German engineers and researchers interacting. It became clear early on that misunderstandings between the two nationalities were due in large part to an ignorance of each other's way of problem-solving, as the following statements make clear:

> *"Germans talk about too many details during the meetings," Americans complained.*

> *"That's not right," countered the Germans, "the Americans don't concentrate enough, don't make real contributions. They don't go to the core of the problem, which means we have to fix up their mistakes afterwards."*

> *During the problem-solving phase, the Americans said that their German boss didn't set "real goals" and left them in the dark, giving neither praise nor critical feedback.*

Analyzing these differences, Schroll-Machl found that, at the outset of a project, Germans showed a greater need for detailed information and discussion. They tended to see the problem-solving process from an engineering point of view, considering all potential problems that might arise and then find the most logical solution. For the German, who unconsciously desires a sense of security and control, achieving a thorough understanding of any problem removes uncertainty and, therefore, anxiety.

During the initial discussion-phase, Germans expected all team members to share their experience and knowledge, i.e. exchanging a lot of detailed information. In turn, this permitted the group to reach a consensus, allowing a more rapid implementation of the agreed-upon strategy. *Schroll-Machl concluded that German decision-making and problem-solving concentrated on the problem, its history and components. Less emphasis was placed on ultimate solutions.*

For the American — less worried, more action-oriented — these initial long discussions were found to be extremely trying (and sometimes boring). They perceived the exchange of too much information as a waste of time, a sort of "paralysis through analysis". No matter how well a plan of action was thought out, it would need to be modified along the way. The Americans often didn't speak up at this stage because they were impatient with such drawn-out discussions. By not saying anything, they hoped to speed up the process and get down to work.

In their minds, problem-solving started out with a short brainstorming session to define goals or mission. They would then devise a series of approximate milestones. *Schroll-Machl found that American decision-making and problem-solving processes were more open-ended, concentrating on defining a goal or vision.*

The Germans felt, that with this sort of approach, the Americans were acting without really understanding the problem, a "mindless actionism" or "cowboy mentality of shooting first and asking questions later". Americans, however thought their approach was more efficient (and creative). In their eyes, the German obsession with sticking-to-the-plan meant being locked into a rigid scheme that didn't allow flexibility during the implementation-phase. Americans continually said they wanted to "keep their options open", perceiving it as a trial-and-error process.

Once a plan was established, German team members were able to go off and work relatively independently on their task. Americans, on the other hand, expected further group meetings and more informal communication throughout. The Germans complained that the Americans asked them needless questions about issues, which, from their viewpoint, had already been discussed and decided in the initial exchanges.

One reason for this communication difference may be the fact that Americans are often given tasks for which they have not really been trained for or because of frequent job rotations, leading to a "learn-by-doing" attitude. With this background, they automatically communicate more with their manager and other team members. Germans, because of their more practical and theoretical training, seem able to work more autonomously than their American counterparts. This is reinforced by the large number of technical rules, standards and company norms, which they are expected to know and follow.

Additionally, Germans unconsciously assume that decisions made at group meetings are binding, whereas Americans see such decisions as guidelines (which can change if the need arises or a better solution presents itself). The fact that Americans expect such changes to happen explains why they are not so interested in detailed analysis early on.

Lastly, because Americans instinctively emphasize the relationship side when communicating, they have a tendency to share more of their personality with co-workers. Germans, who by nature wish to remain credible and objective when communicating, tend to maintain a more impersonal "work only" relationship with colleagues. This explains, in large part, why Americans complain that Germans don't seem to be very open in conversing about a project during the implementation phase.

It is interesting that the nationality of the leader generated different internal dynamics. If the leader is German, the group is more like a coalition. The leader is both an expert — with a detailed understanding of the problems at hand — and a mediator who builds consensus within the group. The German leader is expected to "convince", not give orders. He tends to vote with the group, not decide alone. During the implementation phase, the leader has little interaction with individual group members. Thus, Americans saw him as distant and difficult to reach out to.

The American leader, on the other hand, has a more structured position. He or she is expected to define the middle and final goals, distribute tasks and check to see if they've been done, make decisions. An American leader motivates through intensive communication and offers critical and positive feedback. The dynamics are top-down, a chain-of-command style. During the implementation phase, the American leader is accessible, continuously speaking with all members of the group.

The Schroll-Machl study makes clear that if these differences are explained at the beginning of a joint project, the chances for success increase enormously. However, if cultural awareness is not made a priority and the different communication styles are not understood, German-American projects often fail, causing loss of profits and hurt feelings.

<u>Summary of Differences in joint German-American Teams</u>

Germans	**Americans**
See problem-solving from an engineering point of view; they consider all aspects by spending time on the problem and its history (and less on the ultimate solution).	See problem-solving as more open-ended; they "brainstorm" on how to achieve a desired goal or vision.
Decisions and plans are binding.	Decisions and plans are guidelines.
Find Americans have a "cowboy mentality"; they "shoot first and ask questions later".	Think long German discussions are boring, "paralysis through analysis".
Due to active participation in discussions, can later work more autonomously and need less communication with colleagues.	Don't say much in initial discussions, hoping to speed up process of getting to work, but expect more communication later.
Think Americans ask redundant questions during implementation phase.	Perceive the Germans as impersonal and inflexible during implementation phase.
Group leader was seen as a mediator, expected to integrate differing views by persuasion.	Group leader was seen as the decision-maker, expected to set goals in a top-down manner.

Bibliography

Adler, N.J., *International Dimensions of Organizational Behavior*, PWS-Kent, 1991

Axtell, R.E., *Do's and Taboos of Using English Around the World*, John Wiley & Sons, Inc., 1995

Bailey, George, *Germans: The Bibliography of an Obsession*, The Free Press, 1991

Bennett, M.J., "Towards Ethnorelativism: A Developmental Model of Intercultural Sensitivity", *Cross-Cultural Orientations*, University Press of America, 1986

Chandler, Alfred, *Scale and Scope — The Dynamics of Industrial Capitalism*, Belknap Press, 1990

Craig, G.A., *The Germans*, Penguin Books, 1983

Engel, D., *Passport USA*, World Trade Press, 1997

Flamini, R., *Passport Germany*, World Trade Press, 1997

Francesco, A.M. & Gold, B.A., *International Organizational Behavior*, Prentice Hall, 1998

Guinther, J., *The Jury in America*, Facts on File Publication, 1988

Guy, V. & Mattock, J., *The New International Manager*, Kogan Page Ltd., 1991

Hall, E.T., *Understanding Cultural Differences*, Intercultural Press, Inc., 1990

Hirsch, E.D., *Cultural Literacy*, Vintage Books, 1988

Hofstede, G., "Cultural Constraints in Management Theories", *Academy of Management Executive*, 7(1), 81-94, 1993

Kempe, F., *Father/Land*, Putnam, 1999

Kennedy, P., *The Rise and Fall of the Great Powers*, Random House, 1987

Kohls, L.R. & Knight, J.M. , *Developing Intercultural Awareness*, Intercultural Press, Inc., 1994

Kohls, L.R., *Survival Kit for Overseas Living*, Intercultural Press, Inc., 1996

Larson, R., *Getting Along with the Germans*, Bechtle Verlag, 1989

Lewin, K., Some Social-Psychological Differences between the United States and Germany", *Character and Personality 4* (1936): 265-93

Lord, R., *Culture Shock: Germany*, Graphics Arts Center Publishing, 1996

Mole, J., *Mind Your Manners*, Nicholas Brealey, 1996

Nees, G. *Germany Unraveling an Enigma*, Intercultural Press, Inc. 2000

Otte, M., *Amerika für Geschäftsleute*, Ullstein Buchverlag, 1998

Roland, A., *In Search of Self in India and Japan*, Princeton University Press, 1991

Schroll-Machl, S., "Die Zusammenarbeit in internationalen Teams — Eine interkulturelle Herausforderung dargestellt am Beispiel USA-Deutschland." *Internationales Change Management*, Schäffer-Poeschel Verlag, 1995

Schroll-Machl, S., *Die Deutschen — Wir Deutsche*, Vandenhoeck & Ruprecht, 2002

Stahl, G, Langeloh, C., Kühlmann T., *Geschäftlich in den USA*, Ueberreuter Verlag, 1999

Stewart. E. C. & Bennett, M. J., *American Cultural Patterns*, Intercultural Press, 1991

Tocqueville, A., *De la Démocratie en Amérique*, GF-Flammarion, 1981

Wanning, E., *Culture Shock: USA*, Graphic Arts Center Publishing, 1991

Vlasic, B & Stertz, B., *Taken for a ride: How Daimler-Benz drove off with Chrysler*, HarperCollins Publishers, 2000

Vogel, D., "The Globalization of Business Ethics: Why America Remains Distinctive", *California Management Review*, Vol. 35, No. 1, 1992

Index

About the Author

Patrick Schmidt, an American by birth and education, originally went to Stuttgart for a week-end visit in the mid-seventies and ended up staying 20 years. Through his work as an English teacher for German executives and, later, as editor-in-chief of two German corporate magazines, he became an intimate observer of modern German culture. He is now an intercultural consultant and trainer, specializing in American and German comparative management. He currently lives in Dusseldorf, Germany.

He can be reached by e-mail at: pschmidt.de@t-online.de
or by phone: +49 (0) 211 1709 250

Internet: www.agcc.de